D0950762

"My dear friend Christi Paul truly shows the world what's possible! She bravely shares her journey of making big mistakes, taking responsibility, and creating the life she always dreamed of. If you ever wanted to believe it's possible to move past someone else's limited vision for your life, then this book is for you!"

—**DARYN KAGAN**

(DarynKagan.com), national radio host of *The Daryn Kagan Show and* syndicated newspaper columnist

"I'm a big believer in living with an open heart. It's the only way to live authentically, but it can be frightening, too. Christi's bravery in telling her story isn't lost on me, but what touched me most was her battle with herself to hold on to hope when she didn't see any and to recognize the healing power of forgiveness. Her stellar writing and brutal honesty bring you into her pain and invite you to come with her on a journey that proves, whatever your faith, we all have in us what we need to conquer our fears."

—**JANE SEYMOUR**

Emmy- and Golden Globe–winning actress, author, artist, and designer

"It takes a lot of courage to overcome the pain and anguish of emotional abuse—and even more to write about it. Thank you, Christi, for sharing your own personal heartbreak and triumph. It's empowering. I have no doubt it will encourage people to find their strength. Every woman should read this book!"

—**CHERYL BURKE**

ABC's *Dancing with the Stars* and author of *Dancing Lessons: How I Found Passion and Potential on the Dance Floor and in Life*

"Life can be full of hardship and place seemingly insurmountable obstacles in our paths, and it certainly does not go according to 'our plan.' This one thing, however, is true: God has a plan, even when we don't. Christi's book is a wonderful guide to overcoming those obstacles and living the life we are meant to live."

—NANCY GRACE

Host of HLN's *Nancy Grace* and *Dancing with the Stars* final-five contestant (season 13)

CHRISTI PAUL

HLN AND *In Session* NEWS ANCHOR

Love Isn't Supposed to Hurt

a memoir

FOREWORD BY
DR. SANJAY GUPTA,
CNN CHIEF MEDICAL CORRESPONDENT

Tyndale House Publishers, Inc.
Carol Stream, Illinois

Visit Tyndale online at www.tyndale.com.

TYNDALE and Tyndale's quill logo are registered trademarks of Tyndale House Publishers, Inc.

Love Isn't Supposed to Hurt

Designed by Jacqueline L. Nuñez

Some of the names in this book have been changed out of respect for the privacy of the individuals mentioned.

Library of Congress Cataloging-in-Publication Data

Paul, Christi.
  Love isn't supposed to hurt / Christi Paul.
    p. cm.
  ISBN 978-1-4143-6737-8 (hc)
1. Paul, Christi. 2. Christian biography—United States. 3. Christian women—Religious life. 4. Wife abuse—United States. 5. Wife abuse—Religious aspects—Christianity. 6. Television news anchors—United States—Biography. I. Title.
  BR1725.P274A3 2012
  248.8′6092—dc23
  [B]   2012003019

Printed in the United States of America

18   17   16   15   14   13   12
7   6   5   4   3   2   1

To my cherished daughters, Ava Isabella, Sofia Faith, and Sadie Ruth:

You are strong, creative, compassionate, and brave. God is gonna do great things through you. In fact, He already has.

I am so blessed to be your mom. Thank you for all you are. You are loved beyond words.

Contents

Foreword

WHEN MY DEAR FRIEND Christi Paul first talked to me about writing a book a couple of years ago, we were sitting next to each other in the makeup chairs at CNN headquarters. It was early morning, and while the rest of us were still waking up, Christi was already a bundle of energy. One of my favorite parts of the day was the impromptu discussions I had with Christi.

On that day I was running off to do my show and Christi had hers, so we didn't have as much time to chat. I asked her what she planned to write about. She paused for a while, and for a brief moment her trademark megawatt smile disappeared from her face. "It will be about hope," she eventually answered. That sparked a discussion we have continued ever since. I told her that when Pandora opened the box, many evils escaped—including pain, anguish, and misery. But as some versions of the mythology go, one evil didn't make it out.

"Forbearance," I told her. "We never know what the future

holds, and that provides the greatest hope of all." It is a quintessential human ingredient, and without it, we would be a very different species.

I could tell that my comment hit the mark with Christi, but until I just finished reading her wonderful book, I wasn't entirely sure why. I had heard when this beautiful woman started at CNN that her previous life had been a difficult one, and as a polite colleague, I never wanted to intrude. I was, however, always curious about what had happened to her and shaped her into the person she is now.

Over the years Christi had three daughters and I had three daughters, all around the same age. That cemented our friendship even more. I would laughingly inquire about her husband's sanity, being outnumbered by gals in the house. More seriously, I would talk to Christi about the hopes, dreams, and aspirations she had for her own girls. It seemed I was always trying to learn the best ways to care for my own daughters. Now, after reading this book, I realize Christi provided me an important gift to pass on to my girls—life lessons we all wish we had learned earlier.

To be honest, at the beginning this was a tough book to read. I was learning some awful details about my friend Christi's life, things she had never shared with me or many other people. As I read each chapter, I was worried about her safety, and I worried that she would be too broken and too battered to fulfill the life she deserved to have. Even though I knew the outcome and realized that Christi had persevered through some very tough times, I could not stop reading to learn exactly how she did it. I also realize this was exactly why she wanted me to read it. After all, she had once told me, "It will be about hope." And she really delivered.

The book is about more than that, though. It is about unexpected lessons, taking control of your life, and digging deep to find your courage. At times, the book will challenge your faith—even trash it—as you hear what Christi endured. But in the end she brilliantly always comes back to that galvanizing theme of hope.

Most of us work with colleagues every day and even become friends with them without knowing who they really are or where they came from. That all changed when I read *Love Isn't Supposed to Hurt*. Having written books myself, I know it is scary to put yourself out there for the world to see—and to be vulnerable about some of the most delicate details of your life. Christi was both courageous and brilliant in the telling of her story.

Regardless of your own faith or system of belief, you will learn how the beautiful woman you see on TV every day chose to rely on her own faith and how she turned real tragedy into genuine triumph. After you read the book, hopefully you will get a chance to share it with those you love. At the right time, I will share these stories with my own daughters.

—Sanjay Gupta

Acknowledgments

My parents, Roger and Ann:
Thank you for giving me a home where I could make mistakes and not pay for them all my life, a foundation to know I wasn't only your child but also God's child, and a sense that, no matter what happened, there was a purpose for me.

My Gram Ruth Paul:
I'm sorry we both have this kind of pain in common. I'm grateful we both have our gumption in common. Thank you for showing me you can have a beautiful, purposeful, joyful life with or without a man beside you.

My Gram Ruth Long:
Thank you for always being there for me—with cinnamon toast, a glass of milk, and an "I love you."

Jody, Wesley, and Frederick Paul and my aunts, uncles, and cousins:
I am so blessed to be part of your family.

Danny Paul:
Thanks for getting in just enough trouble every once in a while to take the heat off me. And thanks for letting me lean on you, little brother. I love you.

Nanette Cole Eonta and Jennifer Tibboles Mills:
Thank you for being the sisters I never genetically had. You've held me up when I was ready to crumble, cheered me on when I was trying to fly, and made me laugh until my sides split. Your love, laughter, and loyalty have been the best examples of what true friends are. Thank you. My heart is full.

Carey Pena, Colleen Favetti, Samantha Mohr, Daryn Kagan, Asieh Namdar, Linda Stouffer, Kyra Phillips, Stefani Schaefer, Rachel Thibodeau, Melissa Buchanan, and Marcia Bothe:
You're inspirations to me! You show me what's possible, and you share yourselves so openly. I'm a better person for having you in my life.

Heidi Bodine, Greg Copeland, Holly Wendt, Jason Hamilton, and Robin Meade:
Your endless support makes my heart swell. Thank you.

Ben Mira, Duane Meyer, Randy Miller, and Greg Glover:
Thank you for always being my protectors and for your insights into the male mind. You're prime examples of "the good guys" out there. Well, except for your high school antics, but that's a whole other book. Ha! I'm grateful for you always.

Uwe Stender and Kenny Lindner:
Agents extraordinaire! Thank you for your expertise, your guidance, and your fighting spirit. I'm lucky to have you on my side.

Carol Traver:
Your belief in this story and in me still boggles my mind. Thank you for taking a chance to talk about something that's been hidden behind closed doors for far too long.

Stephanie Rische:
You're to a manuscript what a dishwasher is to a glass—your cleaning and polishing make the vital messages transparent. Thank you for helping my voice and my story shine brighter. It's better because of you.

My CNN/HLN/In Session family:

Chuck Roberts, Sanjay Gupta, Nancy Grace, Jane Velez Mitchell, Bill Galvin, Scott Tufts, Tim Mallon, Brad Tachco, Sunny Hostin, Renea Lyon, Tara Hill, Carolyn Disbrow, Alison Rudnik, and our incredible team of talented producers, directors, writers, makeup artists, and fellow anchors—thank you for your ever-present encouragement, words of wisdom, and staunch support! I'm so blessed to be able to work alongside you clever, creative people whom I not only respect but also truly like and appreciate.

Dr. Amelia Case:

Your hours of probing, guiding, cheering, and questioning helped me do something remarkable: thank God for every step and misstep, trust my instincts, and recognize how beneficial every trial and trauma is to making us who we're meant to be. You're an angel, and I'm eternally grateful.

My husband, Peter:

Just like the meaning of your name, you are my rock. Your extraordinary strength, acceptance, compassion, and gut-busting laugh rock my world in the best possible way. No wonder women are always asking me if you have an available brother. You're the best gift God ever brought to my life. I love our mantra in this house when something breaks:

Our girls: Daddy will fix it, Mamma.

Me: Why will Daddy fix it?

All of us: Because Daddy fixes everything [with our hands in the air].

That's true on so many levels. God help the young men our girls date. They have a lot to live up to.

I love you forever.

Prologue

I'M CONVINCED THAT somewhere in the archives of a photography studio in Ohio there is a picture of me I never want to see.

The sun was beautifully bright that August afternoon in Sandusky as we stood in front of a gorgeous garden splashed with flowers. The photographer said, "Go ahead and dip her." My new husband slid his hand around my back, and as he started to dip me, he hissed at me through his smile, which was really just gritted teeth. "When is this going to f---ing be over?"

At that moment the sun was my enemy. It had to be exposing the white of my face as the blood drained out of it.

Could it be? Could my husband of only two hours want that desperately *not* to be in this moment?

I felt like someone had poked a hole through my chest, stuck a straw in the opening, and started sucking the air out of my lungs. No breath came out for a few seconds. Just long enough for the shock to register on my face as the camera flashed.

And somewhere in a closet of that photography studio they

probably have it on a negative they were too kind to ever develop. Thank you, photographer.

But the words were seared into my memory . . . no picture needed. It was at that split second that I thought, for the first but not the last time that day, *Dear God, what have I done?*

CHAPTER I

REMEMBER YOUR ROOTS

DEAR GOD, what have I done?

Of all the things I dreamed of feeling on the day I got married, that was not one of them.

I know. I should have been more honest with myself. By that point in my life I had sat through my share of weddings. If I had lined them up to see how many unions had survived, I'd say I was looking at a 50/50 split—half of the marriages were still going strong, and half had already crumbled. I was a big talker back in the day, too, often proclaiming, "I don't care if I'm standing at the end of the aisle in my dress with everyone seated and ready to go. If it doesn't feel right, I'm not walking down that aisle!"

But that's exactly what I did. Standing at the back of the church, just before the doors opened, with my father by my side, I said,

"Dad . . . you'll always be the number one man in my life." I looked at him, and he was fighting back tears. Thinking back on the day now, I wonder if it was simply because he was facing that moment a father dreads most—giving his daughter away—or if there was more to it. If he, too, was scared. If he knew that this was not how things should be.

It should have been a warning sign to me that when I told him he'd always be the number one man in my life, I truly meant it. You'd think that as I was getting ready to say, "I do," I should have been pledging that spot to my new husband. Or that I wouldn't feel the need to "number" people at all—that I could love both of them without categorization. But, truth be told, the man I was walking toward was not someone who made me feel safe or cherished or authentically loved. I think I just convinced myself of that for as long as I could because it was what I wanted to believe . . . whether it was real or not. And in that moment, despite all my proclamations of "I'll never make that mistake," there I was, walking right into it.

In terms of logistics, everything else was perfect. My most treasured friends were there standing up for me, the church was filled with all the people who were important in my life, and my dear family friend and pastor, Roger Miller, had come back to town to perform the ceremony. I suppose those distractions were enough for me to gloss over the truth that was standing right in front of me.

Roger's message that day was haunting, though I didn't realize it for a few more years. He kept repeating, "Remember your roots. Remember the family you came from that loves you. Remember what makes you who you are. . . . Remember your roots." Maybe he knew too. Maybe he sensed this was not where God meant for me to be. Maybe the message was Pastor Roger's way of preparing me for the journey ahead . . . and giving me some direction to guide me through it. But I'm sure even he had no idea how torturous the journey was going to be.

Of course I'd heard about women who lose themselves completely, who give everything they have to a man, allowing his life to take over. It never entered my mind that I could be one of them.

But in one walk down the aisle, I did just that. And I had no one to blame but myself. I chose it, even though I didn't realize I was doing it.

Isn't that how it always seems to work? One day you wake up, look around, and wonder, *Where am I? Whose life am I living, and how did I get here?* Little pieces of the real you keep flitting away in someone else's wind until the you that you've always known has disappeared. It happens so gradually you don't even notice it at first. I know I didn't.

———•———

A few weeks after the wedding, Justin and I were watching the video of our big day, and I found myself overwhelmed with shame and sadness. I tried to hide it, but I guess my heart was on my sleeve. I can be a darn good actress when I want to be, but the fact is, if I care deeply or if I'm hurt, it shows. My new husband noticed, and he didn't like it.

"What's wrong with you? You're not happy after watching our wedding?" he snapped.

But if you could see the tape, or if you had been at the wedding, you'd know why. It's impossible to ignore Justin's impatience blaring through each scene in the video—the stomping away from the altar when the photographer wanted to take a few more pictures of me alone, the rolling of his eyes when the DJ asked us to dance together again. At one point I heard someone in the background say something to the effect of, "It looks like Christi's initiating all the kissing." I was humiliated. What I had refused to acknowledge before was now right there on tape as evidence, and I couldn't ignore it.

At the beginning of our relationship I wrote off this impatience as simply Justin's personality. That's how he handled a lot of things in his life . . . with eye rolling and a lot of huffing and puffing. But as the years went by, I had to acknowledge that maybe, in his heart of hearts, he didn't want this marriage after all. Maybe he only wanted me with him because he didn't want to be alone. Maybe he had his own insecurities to deal with. Maybe he wasn't ready to get married. Whatever the reason, I hurt for both of us.

Until you acknowledge your contribution to a broken situation, you can't truly start to fix it.

I can't tell you how many times over the next five years I looked back on that day and asked myself, *Where was I?* I was strong! I was smart! I was independent! What alien took over my head and my heart, telling me, *Yeah, walk down that aisle. Marry that guy! That's what you should do?*

I knew when all was said and done, it wasn't only Justin's fault that we'd gotten married. I had made this choice. I'd said yes; I'd walked down the aisle; I'd spoken the words *I do.* And I'd lied to myself about it the whole time. I suppose I wanted to marry him so much that I allowed that desire to override all the trepidations and doubts I had.

But it took me a long time to own my part in it. What's important is that I finally did. Because until you acknowledge your contribution to a broken situation, you can't truly start to fix it.

There was a landfill full of rubbish I had to wade through before I was honest enough with myself to start making some sound decisions, though. Before I could find my way back to the real me—the person God had created me to be. At one point, it all literally brought me to my knees.

But on the night of my wedding, I laid my head down on a pillow, closed my eyes, and prayed, "God, be with us." Quite frankly, I didn't have any other words.

CHAPTER 2

WHEN YOU LOSE,
DON'T LOSE THE LESSON

I MET JUSTIN at my first television job. We were co-anchors in a tiny market in West Virginia—market size 161 out of 210 in the country at the time. Everyone there was a one-man band, meaning we wore every hat imaginable. Reporter, anchor, photographer, editor.

The days were grueling—I'd lug camera equipment through every inclement weather pattern, then scramble to set up the tripod and get the video I needed while simultaneously scouting out the scene to identify (and catch) the people I needed for a sound bite. Since I didn't have any experience in editing, it took me a while to get the hang of it . . . much to the delight of a couple of the girls at the station who knew a lot more than I did. They didn't hesitate to make fun of me—sometimes behind my back and other times right in front of my face. On the worst days, it worked. I felt completely inadequate.

There I was, starting out in television at twenty-six years old—a dinosaur in this business! Most of my colleagues were fresh out of college. But on some level I knew this opportunity had come to me for a reason. I knew I had to grab it with both hands and run with it. And so, as the weeks wore on, I dug in my heels and started getting the hang of things. It was a good lesson for me in putting myself out there at the risk of criticism, in sifting through what other people thought of me and holding it up against what I knew to be true about myself. As it turned out, it wouldn't be my final lesson in that arena.

As much as I would have hesitated to admit it at the time, the small-market experience was a blessing because it taught me to appreciate every position that goes into pulling off a newscast. I learned that it's not about one person—no one can do it alone. It takes a team to put together great stories and impactful news-casts. I'm grateful to have always been surrounded by good teams, starting with that first position in West Virginia. I learned from a group of talented people and was able to be part of some work we were all proud of.

But let's be honest—starting in market size 161 is no one's ideal. I was young and, quite frankly, naive. Although I'd spent a summer in Los Angeles for an internship with *Entertainment Tonight* and had lived on my own in Cleveland for a couple of years, there was some-thing about this move to West Virginia that felt jarring. Unsettling. I'd left a decent position in Cleveland as tourism manager of the Convention and Visitors Bureau to take this job, and it was scary. Sure, I was excited about the change, but it felt like a huge lifestyle shift—moving from the hustle and bustle of the city to the quiet hills of no-man's-land. I found myself in a newsroom that seemed terribly primitive to me—we were still typing on typewriters, and we had to tape scripts together and feed them through a projector for the prompter. On top of it all, I didn't know a soul for a one-hundred-mile radius.

I was truly alone.

I found myself asking, *What if I don't make it? What if I stink at this? If I can't do it, what's next?*

Yeah, insecurity is a pain.

At night I'd lie in bed trying to fall asleep, remembering the look on my mom's face when my parents left me here. After helping move me into my apartment, my parents took me to dinner. I could tell Mom was as anxious as I was. I think we both knew this was a good thing—something I had to do if I was ever going to get to my dream job, which at the time was to be the morning and noon anchor at the NBC affiliate in Cleveland. I remember leaving the parking lot of the restaurant going one way while they turned the other, all the while watching in our rearview mirrors. Once their car disappeared over the horizon, I cried. No, I sobbed. Like a two-year-old. This seemed like the craziest move I'd ever made.

———•———

The news business—especially for someone who's just starting out—is brutal on several levels. For one thing, the competition is fierce. Number two, one-man-band work is exhausting and stressful because there's always a deadline looming. And three, you're sure not going to get rich in those early years.

I did my best to settle in and to focus on doing a good job and learning the ropes so I could eventually move on. I wasn't alone in that goal. All of us at the station were as poor as church mice—most of us had a starting salary of $12,000 a year. Yes, you read that right. No numbers are transposed. Twelve. Thousand. Dollars. That meant some of us were living in parts of town that weren't exactly safe.

One evening I remember the sports guy, Jon, calling to warn me he'd just heard over the scanner that there was a prison escapee alleged to be somewhere in the apartment complex where I lived. The police were on their way, he said. I locked my door and later heard some commotion nearby. They got him.

Our newscast covered topics like city council meetings, local festivals, and the hunting season. There were some perks, though, and those usually came in the form of the people we got to know. Small communities are loyal communities, and the people of Clarksburg were incredibly kind to us. I remember one councilman who would sit through tedious meetings trying to distract me by throwing wads of paper at me or tossing candy to me as the meeting crawled to an end. It was nice to know I wasn't the only one who thought the meetings were hopelessly boring.

There was another plus to starting in a small market: when you make mistakes—and you *will* make mistakes—the whole world doesn't see them. (Unless, of course, it gets posted on YouTube, but that came after my small-market time.)

When we first met, Justin seemed larger than life. Granted, he did have a bit of a temper, but he was charismatic and charming and had so much ambition. He was intensely driven, and I was taken with that . . . drawn to it, even. And while he might not have been patient, he did seem to enjoy taking care of me. That made me feel loved. One night, after I'd gotten sick and couldn't go to work, he called me, just to see how I was doing. Another time, when he knew I was out on a late-breaking story, he came back to the station well after midnight. He saw the lights on at the station, he said, and he wanted to make sure I'd gotten back okay. Yes, Justin had a wonderfully caring side to him.

And I was in a very vulnerable place when I fell into his life.

Far away from my friends and family and still trying to get acclimated to a new place just five months after moving, I was feeling alone and insecure. And things were about to get much worse.

In the early morning hours of Valentine's Day, my phone rang. It was Mom. She started by saying, "Christi, something awful has happened. But I want you to know your dad and I and Danny and the grandmas are all okay." Even as my mind was whirling, I thought about how brilliant she was to instantly halt my visions of something horrible happening to the people I cared for most. She knew me well, and she knew that was where my mind would go first.

"P.A. is in the hospital. He tried to kill himself."

Everything went still as I tried to process what she was saying. I tried to say something, but no words came out.

P.A. was my brother's best friend and basically part of our family. He and Danny had been inseparable throughout high school, and he was even my little brother in our high school production of *The Sound of Music*. I played Liesl and he was Friedrich, so we always joked that he really was my second little brother.

"What happened?" I finally got out.

"We don't know why it happened, honey." Mom went on to say that late the night before, he called Danny, who was three hours away at college. P.A. told him he couldn't take it anymore.

Danny tried to talk to him, to plead with him. But in the end, P.A. simply said, "I love you, man. Fade to black." And he hung up.

After frantic calls from my brother to my mom and P.A.'s family, they heard that a police officer had found P.A. sitting in his car in the high school parking lot. The officer had his lights shining toward him and spent some time talking to him from a distance, trying to get him to think about what he was doing. The officer later told us he saw P.A. lean his seat way back, and then the rear window of the car simply exploded. He'd shot himself.

But P.A. wasn't dead. He was in the hospital in Toledo. Mom said they didn't know how much time he might have, so I knew I had to get to him right away. *How could he have been so desperate that he thought this was the only way out?*

I got dressed, went to work, and walked straight to my news director. "I can stay and do the show tonight," I said, "but then I have to go home."

Here's the thing—it was February sweeps. Anyone in news knows how crucial that time is, especially for the main anchors. I knew there was a possibility my director would say, "If you leave, don't bother coming back." I'd only been there five months, after all. But there was no question in my mind. I was determined to be home—either to support my brother if P.A. woke up or to say good-bye to P.A. if he didn't.

I'd already lost one friend without having a chance to say good-bye. I wasn't about to let it happen again.

Four years before this call about P.A., my friend Melissa was murdered.

The afternoon before Melissa died, I was sitting at home watching the snow fall, and I couldn't shake the feeling that I had to get in touch with her. I just had this sense that she was having trouble with a guy she was newly dating. I picked up the receiver at least half a dozen times to contact her, but I never made the call. I was trying to be sensitive, I guess, thinking if she needed me she'd let me know.

I wish I'd listened to that nagging feeling and called her. I didn't know it then, but it would have been our last conversation.

The next evening a mutual friend called to tell me Melissa was missing.

I called Melissa's apartment as soon as I woke up the next morning. I didn't recognize the voice that answered, but I asked if Melissa was there. There was a pause, followed by the words I will never forget: "Melissa is dead."

I felt all the air being squeezed out of my lungs. Then the questions started charging in my head, one after the other: *What happened? Where was she? Was it an accident?* And the one that sticks around the longest: *Why?*

I slumped onto the couch and buried my head in my hands. Finally, after about an hour, I was able to get a grip on myself enough to turn on the television. Melissa's story was splashed across every news station from Toledo to Cleveland. She had been shot. There was no suspect . . . yet.

In the days that followed, answers started to permeate the fog. Someone had made a call to the police early in the morning, claiming there had been gunshots in a campus parking lot. A witness had allegedly seen a taxi pull away from the area where her body was ultimately found. By the end of the week, campus police officer Jeffrey Hodge was in custody and had admitted to pulling Melissa over, handcuffing her, and eventually shooting her fourteen times. *Fourteen* times.

Hodge pleaded guilty and is now serving a life sentence.

If someone had asked me then what I wanted, I would have said justice. I wanted this guy to pay for his crime, to get what he had coming. It's part of human nature, I suppose. But looking deeper, I guess what I really wanted were answers. It seemed unfair not only that Melissa was taken away from us but also that we didn't know why. I firmly believe in heaven and in God, but in all honesty, when someone is snatched away so violently and abruptly, it's hard to accept that she's in a better place.

Everything we experience— every loss, every torment, every numbing pain—has something to teach us. But we spend so much energy attempting to outrun our agony that we don't take the time to figure out what God is trying to reveal to us through it.

I knew Melissa was no longer suffering, and for that I was grateful. But those of us who remained behind were still haunted by the images that played over and over in our minds.

I tried to keep reminding myself that Melissa's pain was over.

———•———

Melissa's death was a defining moment for me in more ways than one. It was through that experience that I learned to look for the lessons.

"When you lose, don't lose the lesson." I'd heard this expression before, but somehow it wasn't until tragedy struck that it really sank in. This was no longer just a nice saying; it was *true*. Everything we experience—every loss, every torment, every numbing pain—has something to teach us. Something that will make us stronger and wiser. But we spend so much energy attempting to outrun our agony that we don't take the time to figure out what God is trying to reveal to us through it.

It took time, but eventually I gleaned two profound lessons from losing Melissa.

Number one: asking why was useless. I'd been on my knees countless times, pleading with God, "Why did You do this? Why did You allow this? Why didn't You save her?"

There came a day when I finally accepted that those questions were irrelevant. I envisioned sitting with God and asking Him, for the hundredth time, why He hadn't intervened and stopped the bullets. Or brought someone to her rescue. Or kept her away from there in the first place.

As that image of my dialogue with God played in my head, I suddenly realized something: He would never have an answer for me because at the end of the day, there was nothing He could say that I would be able to accept on human terms.

I could choose to be ticked off, or I could choose to trust God.

And being angry about it wasn't going to get me anywhere. I eventually had to learn to trust God in all things, even when they didn't make sense to me. Even in those moments that contorted my mind and challenged every ounce of faith I had. Even in the baffling mystery, the heartbreaking loss, the stifling loneliness.

There are certain things we will never know the answers to in this life. Period.

And somehow, by the grace of God, we have to learn to be okay with that. Life is too short to allow toxic bitterness to make its home in our hearts, gradually eating away chunks of what makes us, well . . . *us.*

So what I learned in the wake of Melissa's death was that I had a choice: I could choose to be ticked off, or I could choose to trust God. Yeah. It's a choice.

Lesson number two: there's a reason for me. And there's a reason for you, too. There's a reason we're still breathing and talking and waking up in the morning. There's a purpose for our words, a destination for our dreams, and an intention for our ambitions. All these things are part of who God made each of us to be.

This world needs you. Even if you may not know why at the moment.

Circumstances are some of the biggest liars of this world. When trauma strikes—when our bodies become ill or our relationships start to disintegrate or a friend betrays us—we wonder if there is still a purpose for us. We confuse the situations we've been handed as indications of how much—or how little—God loves us. But one doesn't equate with the other.

Your purpose isn't connected to how worthy you feel. It's connected to God's grace. You may not be able to identify your purpose, but that doesn't mean God isn't working behind the scenes, moving the game pieces around to bring it to you. In those moments, your only job is this: keep the faith. Hold on to hope. And don't let tough times steal your joy. That, too, is a choice.

And so, through Melissa's death, I chose to believe I had a God-given purpose—something he had created me specifically to fulfill.

There was a third lesson too: that every good-bye counts. I had missed my good-bye with Melissa. I wasn't about to miss it with P.A.

Fortunately, my news director was understanding. Without blinking an eye, he said, "Go home, Christi."

I made it back in time to sit by P.A.'s hospital bed. I held his hand and told him he'd always be my second little brother. He lay there, unable to move or talk or even open his eyes, but whenever we talked to him, he'd start breathing a little heavier and his heart rate would go up. I'd whisper something to him and then watch for any sign of movement. Though there were no outward responses, the lines on the monitors would flutter every time. It was comforting to know he could hear us.

After a couple of days, he was taken off the machines. I ache to think that as he lay there, unable to move or communicate, he was probably wishing he could take it all back. Wishing he would have chosen differently that night. It's what we all wished.

And there it is again—that profound lesson about choices. Once we make them, we're tied to them, and the consequences will follow us. But we also need to know that each day we get the chance to choose all over again. And believe me, there's hope in that.

I was about to make one of the biggest choices of my life—to get married. And the consequences, I would soon find out, would be steeper than I ever imagined.

CHAPTER 3

BEING ANGRY
DOESN'T GIVE ANYONE
LICENSE TO BE CRUEL

JUSTIN AND I started dating the week after P.A. died. You might be keen enough to see where this is headed. If so, you're a step ahead of where I was at the time.

After all that had happened, Justin seemed to be the place of comfort and security I was looking for.

———•———

There had been an undercurrent of sparks between us after several months of working together. We often hung out after the shows, grabbing a bite to eat with the gang. He was a classy guy—nice to everyone, always including people. He had a quick wit—a kind of dry sense of humor where he would make fun of someone in a way that didn't seem demeaning, just comedic. And he had a good sense of style.

One night when we were out, I looked at him as he was talking to a colleague, and I suddenly realized how handsome he was. His sandy brown hair was a little mussed up, and his navy wool coat was unbuttoned and hanging over his shoulders. His khaki pants hung just to the edge of his loafers.

Our eyes locked for a second, and we just smiled at each other. We both knew something was happening between us, but we weren't sure where it was going. The day before Valentine's Day, Justin took advantage of the holiday and amped it up. Nothing official had happened between us yet, but I think we could both feel it coming. I opened the door of my apartment to find a beautiful bouquet of roses. It simply said, "Thinking about you. Love, Justin." My heart swelled as I placed the flowers on my dining room table and stared at them.

I wasn't sure I was ready for this. My plan when I came to West Virginia was to work my tail off and then move on to a bigger market. I wasn't there to find love. But it seemed it was finding me, whether I was looking for it or not.

All thoughts of roses, Valentine's Day, and love were put on hold, though, when I got the call about P.A. the next day.

As I was driving to Ohio, my phone rang. It was Justin, calling to check on me. "Are you okay, Christi? Is the drive home going all right?" It was evident that this man cared about me, that he wanted to be there for me. And that felt good at such a vulnerable time.

After P.A.'s funeral I returned to West Virginia, and Justin and I started dating. We spent almost all our time together outside work—going to movies, going out for dinner, attending get-togethers with friends and colleagues.

One day we were in his apartment cleaning up for a party he was hosting. The radio was blaring as I set things out in the kitchen and he tidied up the living room. Just then one of my favorite songs came on: Natalie Merchant's "Wonder." Justin knew I loved it. He grabbed my hand, pulled me over to him, and danced with me right there in the living room. Together we belted out, "They say I must be one of the wonders of God's own creation!" It was such a tender moment . . . holding hands and dancing around as we sang to each other. I laughed at the way he shook his shoulders up and down and spun me around. I felt like he was singing all those words directly to me—that I was his "wonder." With the sting of P.A.'s suicide still so raw, I wanted to do all I could to hold on to the people who mattered to me. And there was no doubt now that Justin mattered to me.

A couple of months later, Justin interviewed for a job in Boise, Idaho. The night after he returned, he took me to dinner, and as we sat in the booth, I listened to him gush about the station there and the people he'd met. He was sharp and determined, and I knew Boise would be lucky to have him. For his part, Justin was hopeful about his chances of landing the position.

As I was processing all he was telling me, he suddenly dropped something that nearly made me fall out of my seat. He squeezed my hand and looked into my eyes.

"I don't want to go to Boise without you," he said. "If I get this job, I'm going to ask you to marry me."

I was stunned. We'd been dating only four months! But when I thought about it, I didn't like the idea of being without him, either. As I went home that night, I couldn't quiet the thoughts swirling in my head. *Can I go to Boise with him? Can I walk down the church aisle and marry him?* Was I ready? Was he? I didn't know for sure, but I knew I was happy to have him in my life. Happier than I'd been in quite a while.

I was sitting at a table in the break room the next night when Justin walked in and pulled up a chair next to me.

"I got the call," he said.

"*The* call?" I asked.

"Yeah. I'm going to Boise!" He was beaming.

"Oh my gosh! Congratulations!" I hugged him tight.

When I pulled back to look at him, I saw tears in his eyes. I had never seen such a tender look on his face. Then he took my hand and said, "Will you go with me?"

For the sake of full disclosure, I have to tell you that I hesitated for a minute. For one thing, I wasn't really sure what he meant. Was this a marriage proposal? He didn't say it formally, but I guessed it was. He'd told me the night before that he wanted to marry me and take me with him.

I just sat there looking at his eyes, still full of tears and love, and after a couple of seconds I gave the only answer that seemed possible to me at the time. I said yes.

About an hour later I was on the phone with my mom. "I think I'm getting married and moving to Boise!" I said.

"Whaaat?"

You can imagine the jolt that was for her—and for the rest of my family and friends. This was all happening so fast. Most of them had never even met Justin.

I barely blinked, and that tiny snowflake of a moment that had floated between Justin and me in the break room snowballed into something big. A full-fledged wedding.

Over the years I've gotten better at recognizing those moments when God clearly has a hand in things—those moments when He gives us a chance to make a different choice. Some people see those experiences as coincidences or unexplainable circumstances, but I've come to recognize them as a nudging guidance. He allows certain things to come into our lives as a way of leading us toward His will for us or away from something that's not part of His plan. And how have I learned this lesson? Mostly from the times I failed to listen.

This was one of those times.

Several days after Justin and I got engaged, I was in my apartment packing up my things to move to Boise when the phone rang. It was the news director from the NBC affiliate in—of all places—Cleveland. He offered me their weekday morning and noon anchor position. The money was twice what Justin would make in Boise, and it was, by all standards, an incredible opportunity. It would be a jump from market size 161 to 13 at the time. And for me, it was nothing short of a dream come true. This was the job I'd been working toward ever since I got into the business—in Cleveland, at that very station I'd hoped for, as the morning and noon anchor. And on top of that, I'd be close to my family and friends. I was on cloud nine.

But . . . what about Justin? Would he agree to go with me? I had already told him I'd go to Boise.

I told the news director in Cleveland I had to think about it—that I'd just gotten engaged and this would significantly rattle

God allows certain things to come into our lives as a way of leading us toward His will for us or away from something that's not part of His plan.

our plans. He was understanding and told me to let him know by the end of the week.

A few hours later I found myself sitting on Justin's couch in complete confusion. My cloud nine immediately turned dark when Justin flatly refused to go with me. He offered no congratulations, no excitement on my behalf. Just anger.

"How could you even consider it?" he shouted. "We've already made our plans!"

"But, Justin, if I was ready to pack up and go to Boise with you, why won't you consider making a move for me? Surely you could get a job in Cleveland once we got there!"

His words blasted me. "I've already accepted the job in Idaho! I can't renege now! If you want to take the job in Cleveland, go ahead. But we'll be finished! There's no way this will work long distance."

I don't remember what else he said as his yelling tirade continued. But I do remember, after listening to him rant as long as I could handle, I finally jumped in. "Justin. I don't need your criticism right now! I need your understanding."

He quieted down then. "I'm sorry," he said. "You're right. But why can't you just come with me like we planned?"

He never said it outright, but it was obvious I had a choice to make. The man . . . or the job.

Back at my apartment I stared at the moving boxes, half-packed. I could easily move them all to Cleveland rather than Boise. I thought about what it would be like to be near my friends and family again. I could get a cute little apartment, volunteer to do some charity work, and take the job I'd always dreamed of. *What would it be like,* I wondered, *to wake up my parents each morning from their TV screen?*

Then my mind shifted to Boise. I pictured getting a place to live with Justin and wondered whether I'd be able to find a good job in television there. After weighing all the pros and cons, one thing became clear to me: there were many reasons to go to Cleveland. Justin was the only reason to go to Boise.

For four excruciating days I vacillated about it. *Do I choose the job? Or do I choose the man?*

———•———

I remember sitting in my bed one morning as the end of the week crept closer and closer. I knew my window for accepting this job was getting smaller with every tick of the clock.

I thought about P.A. and how short life is. What did I really want? Did I want a career, or did I want to be married to this man I'd fallen in love with? I could feel my heart leaning more toward Boise. But I couldn't ignore one glaring trepidation about Justin: his anger. Sometimes when he flew off the handle, his cursing got out of control, and his tone was so venomous it rattled me. I'd only seen it in full force one time. That should have been enough, but I wanted to give him the benefit of the doubt. We all have bad days, right? That's how many of us tend to rationalize bad behavior, not knowing we'll end up paying for it later.

It had happened one night in the newsroom, before Justin and I were even dating. There was a heated discussion between Justin, one of our producers, and me. I don't even remember what the argument was about, but at one point I stood up and said, "Okay, look, this is crazy. I'm sorry. I didn't mean to yell." Then I looked directly at the producer and said, "I'm sorry." Then I turned around to Justin, who was in an edit bay. "Justin, I'm sorry," I said.

He turned around, pointed at me, and screamed, "F--- you!" with a poisonous edge I'd never heard before.

The producer and I were both in shock. She stepped in. "Hey! Enough, Justin!"

He simply turned his back to us, mumbling something under his breath. I didn't know what else to do besides walk away. I'd never seen anyone react like that before—and certainly not to an apology.

This scenario was nagging me now, the night before I had to give my decision to the NBC affiliate. Justin and I were sitting on his couch, and I felt like I needed to bring it up. "You know, Justin, the one thing that worries me is your anger. I can't forget that night you cursed at me in the newsroom. I don't understand why you get so enraged sometimes, and I don't want to be the target of that kind of hostility. I don't deserve it."

"I know, and I'm sorry about that," he said. "I was just stressed out. It won't happen again. I promise."

He said all the right words. But the thing was, he wasn't looking at me. His eyes were darting all around the room.

The choice was right there in front of me. The job . . . or the man.

You guessed it. I chose the man.

Years later I realized I'd made that decision partly out of fear. The fear of being alone. The fear that Justin was right— we wouldn't make it if I took the job. So on some level I went with him not because I believed we would always be together but because I feared we wouldn't be if I didn't go.

Not quite the picture of emotional health, huh?

But I also married him because I loved him. And I thought he loved me. In my mind, that outweighed any opportunity Cleveland could offer.

The next thing I knew we found ourselves in a whirlwind of engagement parties and wedding plans and preparations to move to Boise.

Shortly after we moved, a weekend anchor position became available at the station Justin worked for. I got the job.

I tried to convince myself that everything was working out. I was in Boise, I had a job, and I was getting married in two months.

There was, however, a red flag that I summarily dismissed. Perhaps when we have our eyes fixated on what we want at the end of the rainbow, we can miss the fact that the rainbow may be lacking a few key hues—colors that we need to see if we ever expect to get to the pot of gold. Those dark pockets should serve as warning signs that maybe this isn't the pathway to treasure, like we assumed. But try telling that to a woman who's determined to get what she wants.

The red flag that hit during our engagement was Justin's refusal to take "the class"—that course required by many churches that helps couples prepare for scenarios and conflicts they're likely to encounter in their marriages. Justin wouldn't answer questions for the pastor about expectations for marriage, how we'd raise kids, how we'd decide whose career to follow, how we'd divvy up responsibilities—from who pays the bills to who takes out the trash.

Justin told me, "I'm not going to sit there and let some pastor guy I don't even know tell me about my own relationship. It's a bunch of bull----."

The more I encouraged him to do it, the harder he fought back. Finally I gave up.

I wondered what he was so afraid of. Why was he so dismissive of this idea? I started to wonder if there was some pain from his past that he wasn't willing to acknowledge. And as crazy as this sounds to me now, I wanted to—wait for it—fix it!

I don't know what it is about women—maybe it's our maternal instinct—but most of us want so badly to make the men we love happy and to heal whatever hurts they carry with them. Women are strong. This is a fact. We can hold down the fort, bring home the bacon, and yes, fry it up in a pan. We believe we can show a man the happiness and trust he hasn't experienced before. At its core, this drive to nurture is a good thing—a God-given wiring. But it can have a dark side too—it can blind us to warning signs we'd recognize under other circumstances.

I think this is when I learned to live in denial, where it started creeping into the very foundation of our relationship. Denial began gradually, so slowly that it was almost imperceptible at first. It crept in as it usually does—inch by inch, piece by piece—until before I knew it, I was submerged in a calamity I didn't even see coming.

I was becoming a woman I never wanted to become—a woman filled with fear and the stubborn pride that I would make things work, despite the signs of anger and inflexibility I saw.

A couple of months later, I married him.

———•———

The occasional glimpses of anger I'd seen in Justin suddenly started to show up more. Even our honeymoon wasn't immune to his outbursts. One night we got in a fight—about what, I don't even recall—and he ended up sleeping on the couch. Hello? On our *honeymoon*! Where was I to go from there?

Starting on our wedding day, it felt like our relationship was on a pendulum, constantly swinging wildly from calm to drama. From laughter to fury.

But things exploded in full force just two months after we got married. That's when I started to truly see a man I didn't recognize.

Justin came home drunk after being out with the guys. I was livid that he was smashed and that he'd driven himself home.

"You could have killed yourself or someone else," I told him sternly.

I had no idea my own anger would launch something in him I'd never seen before. A rage I didn't know existed made its first of many appearances.

He started screaming at me that I didn't really love him. That I was a liar like all the rest of them (whoever "they" were, I didn't know) and that this marriage was over.

"I never want to see you again unless it's in a courtroom!" he screamed.

I froze. No one had ever spoken to me like that before. I'd never experienced such direct cruelty. I felt wholly unprepared to defend myself.

But he wasn't finished yet. He called me a slut and a whore and dropped the f-bomb like he was armed with a truck full of vulgar ammunition. I'd never been called those names before, and I never could have fathomed I would hear them spewing from the mouth of my *husband*. Each word hit me with nearly physical force. *Whore*. It felt like a vacuum was sucking the air out of my lungs. *Slut*. A fist to my gut. And then there was the worst one yet: the *c*-word. Yeah, you know the one. I can't even stand to type it. His accusations felt like a screwdriver to my chest, puncturing everything I thought I knew about myself, then turning and twisting further to convince me I was worthless . . . nothing more than trash he was ready to dump out.

I stood there, dumbfounded. Then, to my horror, he started throwing clothes in a suitcase.

"I'm leaving!" he screamed. "I never want to see you again!"

I made the mistake of trying to talk to him logically at first. Now, if you've ever attempted to have a rational conversation with someone who's had too much to drink, you know my obstacle there.

"Where is this coming from? What are you talking about?" I gasped.

He responded by hurling more insults at me, accusing me of being unfaithful.

Okay. Reason was not working. Next I found myself pleading with him.

"Please, Justin. I don't understand! Please calm down."

Then it happened. *Boom! Boom!* The sound of splintering wood. I looked over, and there were two holes in the bedroom door the size of his fist. He took off his wedding ring and threw it at me. Then he punched a wall. I just stood on the other side of the room, terrified to get too close to him. What if he decided to go from the wall . . . to me?

In the middle of this whole fiasco, one of our old friends from the station in West Virginia called. I answered, and he could immediately hear the commotion in the room and the fear in my voice. I said I'd call him back.

When Justin finally passed out on the couch three hours later,

I took the phone into the bathroom and curled up in the fetal position on the floor. I slowly dialed the number.

"Christi, what happened? What's Justin mad about?" Our friend seemed as stunned as I was.

"I don't know! I have no idea." The words came out between sobs and gasps for air.

I had no answers.

I felt utterly torn. On one hand, I was furious. *I will not let him treat me like this again,* I promised myself. Why had I allowed myself to be someone else's emotional punching bag for the past three hours? Is this what I'd moved my entire life around for?

But on the other hand, I had made a commitment—to God, to Justin, to myself. I had a ring on my finger, after all. It would have been different if I'd been dating him and could just walk away. But I'd always believed marriage is sacred. I had a responsibility here—to give this relationship all I had. To fight for it. To fight for him. To fight for *us*. For better or for worse.

I sat there in the corner of the bathroom, trying to dissect what had just happened. And in that half hour or so, empathy kicked in. I'd seen this man be compassionate. I'd witnessed him care for people who were hurting and celebrate people's joys with them. There had to be an explanation for his behavior tonight.

That's when I came to the conclusion that at some point someone must have hurt Justin so badly that he was taking it out on me. Somewhere in the fog of his past he'd been so wounded that he couldn't process it in a healthy way. Maybe he had never known lasting love before—maybe he'd never had the security of someone sticking around and saying, "I'm not going to leave." Whatever the cause, this man I'd married—this man I loved—was hurting.

And I felt sorry for him.

That's when I decided I needed to prove to him that he could count on me. *This is my husband,* I thought. *I'm his wife. I cannot abandon him.*

I had made my resolution. But that didn't change the fact that I spent that night curled up in a ball, feeling violated and frightened.

———•———

The next morning I decided to face my fear head-on. When Justin woke up, I sat down next to him and said, "I can't live like this, Justin. I don't deserve what happened last night. I can't live with that kind of disrespect and listen to those threats."

"I know," he replied.

"But you need to know that I'm here. I'm not going anywhere. I love you, and I want this to work."

"So do I."

"Can you tell me what happened?" I asked. I was trying to tread lightly. "Why would you accuse me of cheating on you? Did something happen while you were out?"

"I just had too much to drink. That's all," he said. "It's nothing. I'm sorry. I didn't mean to hurt you."

It was clear that no amount of prodding was going to get me anywhere. Justin was only getting more agitated as we talked, so I backed down. The fear of a second round washed over me, and I sat there silently as he got up to shower.

Part of me wanted to walk out. But he was my husband. Not my boyfriend. Not an acquaintance. My husband. I coupled that commitment with a fistful of hope that this wouldn't happen again.

We did have moments of light and laughter during that first year. There were some wonderful days spent giggling together and poking innocent fun at each other, going to movies, hanging with our friends. We had a sweet first Christmas together, too, decorating the tree and attending holiday parties.

One thing that touched me was the effort he put into gift giving. The gifts weren't particularly elaborate or expensive, but they were thoughtful. For instance, he surprised me with a purse I'd admired at a store while on our honeymoon, and he got me a book by Point of Grace, my favorite Christian music group (music that he himself didn't listen to but knew I enjoyed). I was moved by the effort he'd made to search for things he knew would mean something to me.

But our good days were punctuated by drunken stupors: Justin coming home, ripping the covers off the bed as I slept, and screaming at me to get out. One time as he was yelling at me, I started crying and walked into the living room to get away from him. He stormed after me and then, to my horror, egged me on to cry harder. As I sat there curled up on the couch, he hovered over me. "Oh, come on," he mocked. "You can do better than that! Cry harder, baby. . . . Cry harder!"

He was like that redheaded kid in *A Christmas Story*—the bully who follows Ralphie home, tormenting him.

Only I wasn't Ralphie. I didn't have that switch where suddenly rage took over and I was compelled to attack my aggressor, tackling him to the ground and punching away at him.

Instead, I sat on the couch in utter shock. I didn't cry harder—in fact, I stopped crying altogether. I was so taken aback by what

Justin was saying, I could only stare at him. *Who is this man?* I wondered. *This is not the Justin I fell in love with.* This wasn't the man who used to call to make sure I got home okay in bad weather. Who I once overheard gushing to his friend about me. Who said he loved having me around. Who was this person in front of me?

I looked him in the eye. "Why, when I'm obviously hurting, would you intentionally hurt me more?"

He immediately got a pensive expression on his face. Silence. Then he spoke: "Touché."

Just that one word. Then he walked into the bedroom, crawled into bed, and went to sleep.

He never apologized.

I sat in the living room for a long time. What should I do? I considered going to counseling. But in the past when I'd brought it up with Justin, he refused to go. Would it do any good if I went by myself?

Should I stay? Go? I knew I couldn't continue like this. But if I left, how would I explain it to my family? My friends? Our coworkers and boss? And where would I go? I'd have to stay in Boise because that's where my job was. How could I move out and then go to work and face Justin every day? Besides, my dad had just spent all that money on a wedding. And most haunting of all, I'd made a commitment before God and everyone I loved that I fully intended to be forever. How could we call it quits now? We'd been married only four months!

My soul was numb. There might as well have been a vacancy sign hanging around my neck—I felt like an empty shell of the person I used to be. I was too afraid to let myself feel anything.

But I wasn't ready to give up. The next morning I confronted

Justin as diplomatically as I could. I used *we* instead of *you*. I made it our problem, not his problem, hoping he'd realize what this was doing to both of us.

"We don't fight fair, Justin, and we have to learn to do that. I'm in this for the long haul. I'm your wife. But I don't deserve what happened last night. If you're upset about something, let's talk about it. But when you're angry, even when you have a right to be, that doesn't give you license to be cruel to me."

"I know. I'm sorry. I don't know what happened last night, but it won't happen again." His usual response. I sensed no remorse in his voice—no real desire to change.

Inside I was fuming. I felt like he was just saying what I wanted to hear so I'd shut up. Was he really sorry? I didn't know. Could he guarantee that this wouldn't happen again? I wasn't convinced. It was like he was choosing anger as a way of life—as if it would protect him from something. But I knew it wouldn't. It would only expand the fracture that was growing between us. I didn't know how to make it better because I didn't even know what he was really angry about.

I did know, however, why I was angry. I was hurt and scared. And it was starting to feel like God was abandoning me. As desperately as I'd been praying for help, things weren't getting any better.

But my anger was drowned out by fear. I was terrified that if I pressed things further, I'd spark a repeat of the night before.

Yes, fear won out. Again.

I managed to shut down my voice, but I couldn't erase the nagging in my head. Something was very off here.

If we're honest with ourselves, we know when something isn't right. We feel it in our bones—if we allow ourselves to feel, that is. Maybe that's why we work so hard to ignore our emotions. Sometimes it's just easier to shut down than to admit that our choices have brought us to a place of feeling unsafe or insecure or unloved.

And if our attempts to reach out are met with rejection, it only adds to the emotional deadening. If we try to make things better, to offer a hand, and our efforts are rejected, we feel the pain. The thing is, unless we're willing to examine that pain, we start collecting bricks to build a wall around ourselves—a barricade that will help us avoid feeling anything. We think this will be our protection. But it's really just the beginning of hope depletion.

Unless we're willing to examine our pain, we start collecting bricks to build a wall around ourselves—a barricade that will help us avoid feeling anything. We think this will be our protection. But it's really just the beginning of hope depletion.

I hadn't gotten to that point yet, but I was well on my way. Ironically, I was doing exactly what Justin had apparently already mastered: transforming my hurt into anger and using that fury to construct a fortress no one could pass through.

I felt myself starting to pull away from him, and I recognized the danger in that. I was ready to get help—I wanted to sit down and talk it out with him. But I couldn't force him to do that.

So I employed a new tactic: I decided to start giving more respect to this marriage myself. I believed God had made both this man and me with inherent value. If this relationship was going to last, something had to be done to reflect that.

Maybe if Justin saw that I treated him with dignity, I'd get some back.

But as the months wore on, there were several more blowups. One night things went further than I ever imagined possible.

Again, Justin came home after being out with the guys. I was in bed because I had to work early the next morning.

He flew in and ripped the covers off me. "Get out, whore!" he snarled.

As he kept yelling, I got out of bed and went into the living room, trying to get some distance from him. He followed me. Then he grabbed my arms with an iron grip and swung me around to look at him. He was still screaming.

"Stop it, Justin! You're hurting me!" I cried.

The more I tried to wiggle away, the harder he gripped. He shoved me around, clenching his fingers more tightly around my arms. His fingers bore harder into my skin until finally I stopped fighting. And then all at once he chuckled, plopped down on the couch, and eventually passed out.

I went back into the bedroom in a fog. What had just happened? I rubbed my hands over my arms, trying to take the sting out of where he had grabbed me. I got back in bed, just grateful not to be lying next to him.

———•———

The next day when I got home from work, I walked into the bathroom to wash my face. As I reached for the towel, I saw them. Bruises. Black-and-blue finger marks wrapped around my triceps.

I blinked to get a better look. Surely I was seeing things!

But there they were—four dark marks on my right arm, two on my left.

I reached my right arm over my head, examining it more closely in the mirror. That's when Justin walked in. I was startled, but I could tell he'd spotted them too. Our gaze locked for a second, and I saw that tears were welling up in his eyes. Then he turned around, his head hanging low, and walked out without a word.

I didn't know what to say either. I put on my workout clothes and went for a run.

As I crossed the bridge over the river, I stopped and looked at the water streaming between the trees on both sides of the banks. I wanted to jump in. Not to kill myself, mind you, but to swim away. Far away. I wanted to ride the current to a new life—a life where I was free to make choices, free to be myself, free to live out the purpose God had created me for, free to just *breathe*. But I knew that wasn't the answer.

I prayed, "Dear God, please help me. I don't know what to do. This is my husband. I married him. How do I stick with this? How can I help him? How can I make this better for both of us?"

All I wanted to do was leave. But I didn't.

I didn't think anything could rattle me more than the arm-grabbing incident. But just a few months later something happened that terrified me even more.

Justin and I had been out for dinner with several people from work. As the evening went on, Justin proceeded to get plowed. I wasn't drinking at all because with each sip he took, more fear seeped into me. Every time he put the glass to his mouth and swallowed, I found myself getting filled up—not with vodka, but with anger, resentment, and fear.

Things kept escalating until at one point Justin made a joke about me and grabbed my chest—right in front of our coworkers!

Everyone sat there in shocked silence. There wasn't anything funny about it. I was humiliated.

By the time we left, I was fuming. As we drove home, Justin egged me on about how I was no fun, how I must not be happy, and how maybe we should just get divorced.

I was silent. I didn't want to add any fuel to the fire. But it didn't matter—the longer I remained quiet, the more infuriated he got. Finally I had to say something. "Stop it, Justin!" All I could do was hope he'd pass out so I didn't have to deal with his comments.

As soon as we walked in the door of our apartment, he really let loose—hurling vulgarities at me, accusing me of infidelity, and calling me names. He got right up in my face, screaming at the top of his lungs. It was like one of those old military movies where the drill sergeant gets nose-to-nose with his subordinate and launches into a tirade.

My body involuntarily started shaking, and I tried to get away. I tried to bolt, but Justin stepped in front of me, blocking me with his body.

He grabbed my arm again, this time with a force that stunned me. Then he threw me on the bed. When I got up and tried to make a break for the door, he wrapped his hand around the back of my neck, threw me against the wall, and hissed, "I'm going to bash your f---ing head into this wall!"

I stopped breathing momentarily and closed my eyes, anticipating a fist. But instead, I heard a crash in the wall right next to my head. The punch was so close to me that I could feel the swish of his fist as it flew by. It felt like a warning: *Watch out! Next time I might not miss!*

If this was his way of trying to scare me, it worked.

I couldn't deny it anymore—not only had he gotten physical, but now he'd verbally threatened me with more. *Would he do it?* I wondered. I suddenly felt nauseated.

Justin kept me pinned there for a few seconds. When he loosened his grip on my neck, I turned to see his eyes boring into me. I was terrified.

He walked over to the couch and put his head in his hands.

"Please listen to me," he begged.

I stood there, paralyzed. I was afraid to breathe, let alone speak or move.

He said he wasn't happy about the stress of our jobs. He wasn't happy that we were on different schedules so we didn't see each other much. He said he didn't mean what he'd said, that he loved me.

I just kept looking at the floor. I'd heard all of this before. Only this time I had the physical ache in my neck to serve as a jolting reminder of how far he'd taken things this time, and I couldn't shake it off.

After Justin passed out, I called one of our friends from work and told her what had happened. "I just want to leave!"

There, I'd said it. And I meant it.

"I can't do this anymore," I told her. "I need to get out. Can I come to your place?"

She paused, and I heard her sniffle. She was crying. "Are you sure? I really think you should wait until morning and talk to him."

My heart dropped to my gut. I knew I was putting her in a terribly awkward position. She worked with both of us, and while she and I had certainly connected, I could understand why she wouldn't want to get in the middle of this. I guess I just desperately wanted someone to give me permission to leave. Maybe I felt this need so strongly because I'd been married only a few months. Maybe it was because I was living in a new city with a new job and a new husband, and although I'd made some good friends, there was no one close enough—geographically or emotionally—for me to talk to about all this. I was desperate to have someone validate my pain, to agree that I didn't deserve this.

"Okay." I sighed.

She jumped in. "But if he's not better tomorrow, then yes, I think you need to start making some alternate plans and think about your next move. I'll be here for you, and I'm so sorry you're going through this, Christi."

I hung up the phone and looked at my car keys sitting on the table. I wanted to grab them and take off as fast as I could. But where would I go?

It felt like one of those old cartoons I used to watch on Saturday mornings, with the nice twin on my right shoulder and the evil twin on my left.

Evil twin: *You've only been married five months. How could you possibly leave a commitment as significant as a marriage only a few months in? You're not a quitter, are you?*

Nice twin: *You know he didn't mean it. You know he's hurting.*

Evil twin: *But that's no reason for him to abuse you!*

Nice twin: *He'll be sorry in the morning. It'll all work out.*

In retrospect, though, I think it was actually the other way around—the "good" twin was the one egging me to leave, and perhaps that was the best advice. But I wasn't ready to listen.

Aside from the practical issues of not having anywhere to go, there was something else. Truth be told, I still believed in Justin.

Those moments when he was kind, thoughtful, childlike—they were powerful. Those gentle glimpses reminded me of the person I'd fallen in love with, offering hope that the tender, loving side would win in the end.

When you're in the midst of abuse, it's nearly impossible to identify it. You assume it's something that happens to other people but not to you. Sure, rancid words had been hurled at me and fists had flown into the wall and I had bruises again, but I hadn't actually been hit.

There is no justification for ugly words, name-calling, threats, shoving, screaming. It is wrong. It is abuse. And no one deserves that. No one.

This is how we rationalize. Why do we have to absorb a punch to be convinced that this kind of treatment is not acceptable? Where did we learn that, unless a hand smacks our skin, it's not abuse?

But there is no justification for ugly words, name-calling, threats, shoving, screaming. It is wrong. It is abuse. And no one deserves that. No one.

Sadly, I couldn't see that truth yet. Not that evening.

———•———

Later that night as I stared blankly at the lights piercing the darkness from the restaurant across the lake, I had a hideous thought: *I wish he had hit me.*

My eyes started to sting. How grotesque had my life become that I was wishing my husband had hit me?

The thought lasted no longer than a blink, but it was long enough to give a little clarity to the situation. If Justin had hit me, I realized, I could leave with no questions. No one would admonish me for giving up. No one would judge me for walking away. One blow from him would be my out.

But in my mind, since he hadn't hit me, it wasn't bad enough for me to walk.

It struck me then that I was becoming as sick as he was. The moment I found myself wishing that he'd struck me, I realized how warped my sense of self and relationships had become.

I felt completely vulnerable. Devoid of any human value. *How did I allow myself to get here?* I wondered.

CHAPTER 4

THE MOST IMPORTANT THINGS IN LIFE AREN'T THINGS

THE NEXT MORNING I told Justin I couldn't do this anymore. Either we had to go to counseling or this would never work.

"I know it's all my fault," he said. His eyes were red, and he had his head down. "It's not our marriage—it's me."

He admitted he knew it was the drinking. Then, to my shock, he got up and poured a brand-new bottle of vodka into the kitchen sink. I stood there with my mouth open, watching the poison slither down the drain.

"I'll do anything. Whatever it takes," he said. "Because I love you."

It was the first time he promised he'd do whatever it took. The first time he rejected alcohol. The first time he admitted this was his problem.

I clung to the hope that he meant it. And things did get better
. . . for a while.

——•——

We'd made some close friends in Boise. We'd all go to dinner and
baseball games together and host parties at our homes. We also
liked to go skiing up at Bogus Basin. Justin was a much better skier
than I was, and he surprised me with his patience as he coached
me down the hill. I saw glimpses of his sweet, loving side again,
and I soaked it up.

It was around this time that one of the photographers at the
station, Jason, and his wife, Lisa, became dear friends of mine.
They could always make me cackle with laughter, and I felt a real
sense of peace with them. And apparently my ignorance cracked
them up, so we made for a good team.

I remember being in the news truck with Jason on the way to
the Basque festival. Now, mind you, I'm a small-town Ohio girl at
heart, and I hadn't seen much of the world. I asked him, "What's a
Basque?" In response, he busted out laughing so hard the windows
must have shook. I couldn't help but laugh too.

The way I felt with these new friends, especially Lisa and
Jason, posed a striking contrast to the instability I experienced
with Justin. I didn't mind letting my naiveté show with them. It
was freeing to just be myself and not feel afraid to ask questions,
to learn, to admit I didn't know certain things. I knew that while
they might give me some good-natured grief, they weren't criticizing me or berating me the way Justin often did. It was a refreshing
taste of being accepted for who I was.

Despite the relative calm, though, Justin's bouts of anger hadn't completely stopped. And by now I knew his drinking wasn't simply "just out of college" behavior; he had a serious drinking problem. He became a totally different person when he drank. And he was a mean drunk—downright vicious sometimes.

And then a phone call came that gave me some hope: Justin got offered a job in Phoenix.

We were both ecstatic. It meant a bigger market, better money . . . and more important in my mind, the new beginning we desperately needed. While I still hadn't been able to convince Justin to go to counseling, I was seeing a more intentional attempt on his part to control his anger. I had renewed hope that this move would give us a fresh start.

Some friends threw us a good-bye party. We were surrounded by wonderful people in Boise I'd come to cherish, and I knew it would be hard to part ways. Little did I expect, however, that the emotional part of that evening would not be leaving our friends.

I was standing outside with several people when Justin walked out to the corner of the garage and got sick. He'd clearly had too much to drink. When he was done throwing up, we watched him walk back in the house. Through the window we could see him grab another drink.

I started shaking.

By now, whenever I saw that Justin was drinking too much, my body started reacting involuntarily. I tried to hide my shaking hands, but I couldn't keep it from my friends.

"What do you want to do, Christi?" one girl asked me.

I took a breath. "I want to go home," I said. "I want to leave him here."

I was afraid to be alone with him. It didn't dawn on me until later that I was telling these people something that was already quite clear to them.

We all went inside to get my coat and tried to figure out a way to get me to my car without Justin noticing. I was sitting on a bench when another friend of ours, Denise, came up to me and said with a laugh, "Christi, you've got to get your husband out of here. I just walked up to him and said, 'Justin, I'm going to miss you guys!' He told me, 'Well, why don't you take me downstairs and show me how much you're going to miss me?'" She was trying to laugh it off, but her words felt like a fist to my gut.

We decided to employ Denise to distract Justin while I left. We watched from another room as she walked up to him and asked him to go downstairs with her. This was a revealing moment because prior to this, two other people had tried to get Justin downstairs and he'd refused. But when Denise asked, he immediately followed her down the stairs like a puppy going for a treat. My friends looked at me. I could see the sympathy in their eyes, and I knew they could see the humiliation in mine.

I held it together until I got outside and saw several of my friends standing there just looking at me. "Christi, you don't deserve this," they said. "I'm so sorry."

That's when I broke. I bowed my head in my hands, and the tears came in waves.

"I'm so sorry!" I tried to catch my breath. "You've thrown this wonderful party, and I appreciate your support so much. I feel humiliated!"

There was no use denying it now.

That night a girlfriend stayed with me as I cried and tried to sort through all that had happened.

Had Justin cheated on me with Denise? No . . . I didn't think so. But I was pretty sure that was only because Denise wouldn't open that door for him. But Justin? The churning in my gut told me that if given the chance, yes, he would.

Of all the fears I had about Justin, unfaithfulness had never been one of them—until that moment.

Never in my life did I think I'd be the kind of girl who sat up all night with a girlfriend, sobbing and trying to figure out whether to stay with a man who treated me with such disrespect. I knew in my heart of hearts that I was the kind of woman who would leave—if this was a man I was simply dating. But because I was *married* to him, I felt I couldn't abandon that commitment.

And now I found that shame was the cloak I was wearing. It made no sense, really. He was the one who got so drunk he stumbled his way through the house. He was the one who made a fool of himself in front of his friends, drinking until he got sick. He was the one whose actions made people question his faithfulness to me. Yet I was the one feeling the shame.

It took me years to get this, but the problem was that I was interpreting Justin's treatment of me as my worth. It's one thing to sustain a verbal lashing from someone who doesn't really know you or care about you. But it's a complete mind game when that kind of abuse is coming from the one person you're supposed to be able to trust most. At that moment, I didn't know how to separate his treatment of me from my view of myself.

I wondered how much of what I was living was real . . . and how much was a lie.

As I walked around our apartment alone that next morning,

I studied this home I'd tried to create for us. The couch and chairs, positioned just right for conversation and connection. Sterling-framed pictures of our wedding. The crystal bowl we'd received as a wedding gift, full of candy to grab whenever someone passed by. The antique dining set that had belonged to my parents when they got married. The crystal wine glasses in the cabinet alongside the china place settings. These were things that meant so much to me when we received them because they would be part of our home. I'd hoped that moving all of it with us to a new city would help us start over and settle into a new beginning.

But at the end of the day, it was just stuff.

I was surrounded by all these beautiful possessions, but I was living an incredibly ugly life.

"The most important things in life aren't things." I'd read the quote years ago, and it was ringing in my head as I scanned the room, taking in our lovely things. Things I'd tried to fill my life with. Things I'd used to try to distract me from the worthlessness that had settled in. But as I was finding out, the distraction was merely temporary.

I knew right then that I'd trade all of it just to make things right.

No expensive gift could erase the emotional bruises or diffuse my feelings of betrayal. No material possession could fill the void in this marriage or create the stability I craved.

Trust was deteriorating with every tick of the beautiful china clock on the shelf.

A short time later Justin called from our friend's house, where I'd left him.

"What happened?" he asked. "I woke up in a chair facing the corner in the basement! Where did you go?"

"I came home," I told him. "And you can stay there."

"What do you mean, honey?" His voice wasn't convincing. He might not have known exactly what had happened, but he certainly knew it wasn't good.

When I told him how sick he got, how he followed Denise down the stairs, how humiliated I was, he immediately apologized. He blamed it all on the alcohol.

I said, "I've got a few things to do. I'll come get you in a little bit." And I hung up.

I knew I'd have to face this—and him. The reality was, I couldn't just leave him there.

We were married. This was his home too.

But I was, for the first time, really considering not going with him to Phoenix. Yes—this could be my out.

But again, that nagging voice in my head hammered on: *You've only been married a year—are you going to give up already?*

And the truth was, as much pain as I'd experienced in that year, marriage was sacred to me.

I felt like I was in prison. I might as well have been sitting in a tiny, windowless, concrete cell.

I'd stood in that church, in front of everyone who mattered to me, and pledged before God my faithfulness, love, and loyalty to this man. I had made my choice. And now, I figured, I was stuck with it.

I walked out to the deck and stared at the streaks of sunlight splashing against the mountains. The lake was as smooth as glass, and the reflection of the mountains made a perfect mirror image in the water. There I was, living amid this strikingly gorgeous view of the world God had created, and I felt like I was in prison. I might as well have been sitting in a tiny, windowless, concrete cell.

"God, where are you?" I asked.

I took a deep breath and buried my head in my hands. "What do I do, God? Do I stay or do I go?"

It wasn't the first time I'd asked the question, and it wasn't the first time I thought I heard, "Go."

What? I thought. *That can't be right!* Surely God would never tell me to abandon my marriage or this man who obviously needed love and support. No. God wouldn't tell me to leave. I figured I was just translating the yearning in my heart into my head. It must have been my own voice I was hearing. Not God's.

But somewhere deep inside me, I knew. There was a part of me that was even afraid to pray anymore because I was scared of the answer I'd get: that I needed to leave. That answer contradicted everything I'd always believed about marriage.

Then again, so did my husband's behavior.

When I picked Justin up at our friends' house, I couldn't conceal my anger. I said, "You know, you might have cheated on me last night."

"Oh, Christi, I'd never do that!" he exclaimed.

"I don't know that I can be sure of that anymore. There's a lot of trust that needs to be healed here. And it's going to take a lot from you to do it. I'm seriously wondering if I should just let you go to Phoenix yourself."

"What are you talking about? You have to come with me! I'm so sorry! I didn't mean to hurt you! I'd never cheat on you!"

Blah blah blah blah blah.

"You did a lot of damage last night, Justin. I can't just forget this. What you did is not okay."

"I promise what happened last night will never happen again. You're my wife, and I love you," he whispered as he wrapped his arms around me.

But I wasn't nearly as certain of that as he seemed to be.

CHAPTER 5

PEOPLE CAN SAY SOMETHING IN A SECOND THAT TAKES YEARS TO HEAL

WE GOT OFF to a good start in Phoenix, and I felt more hopeful than I had in a long time. I moved to the city jobless, but after several months of freelancing for the ABC affiliate, KNXV, they offered me a full-time contract. In the middle of the contract negotiations, however, something unexpected happened.

My friend Rachel in Chicago had a connection with someone who knew the assistant news director at KTVK, another station in Phoenix. She told him about me, and the next thing I knew I had a phone call from Dennis O'Neill saying, "Hey, I know you're in town. Why don't you come in and we can talk?" He'd seen me on the ABC affiliate as a fill-in anchor and weathercaster.

I chuckle as I write this, because I, my friends, am no trained weathercaster.

When KNXV hired me on a freelance basis, I had to get a

crash course from Ed Phillips, the prime-time meteorologist. He schooled me on how to render the maps, stack a weather segment, and work the computers. The only thing I knew going into this weather gig was that low pressure meant bad weather and high pressure meant good weather. So much for my college education!

One of the producers had boosted my confidence, though, when she told me she'd overheard Ed tell the news director, "Christi is no dumb blonde. This lady knows what she's doing!" For that, I can only give thanks that I've always been surrounded by people who are good at what they do and are willing to share their knowledge.

That said, I went in and met with O'Neill at the other station. He showed me the newsroom and talked about their news philosophy, and we had some great conversations. I was sitting in his office when he called in his fellow news director Phil Alvidrez. Phil had someone with him and was heading out the door, so we exchanged a quick "Hi, nice to meet you," and he was gone.

Years later, O'Neill spilled the rest of the story to me. Apparently, the day after my interview, Phil was in his office watching the monitors during the noon shows, and he saw me doing the weather at KNXV. He bolted into O'Neill's office, pointed at the monitor, and said, "Who is that, and why isn't she working for us?"

O'Neill basically said, "Hey, bonehead, you met her yesterday right here in this office!"

So much for my first impressions, huh?

I was grateful, though, because I needed someone to believe in me right then. With the tumult of my home life in the past year, my self-image was at an all-time low. Both stations started upping the ante on their offers, and I eventually went to KTVK. I had a lot of admiration for the people I worked with at KNXV, but I went with my gut. And it paid off. The people at KTVK were like no other bunch I'd worked with before—it was truly a family atmosphere. I was blessed by this job and these people, and I knew it from the get-go.

On the home front, things got better for a while. Justin embraced his new job at another station, and I started to let down the wall I'd been building around me. We went to the movies and out to dinner, and we explored this new city we called home. I felt like we were on a whole new adventure. Justin and I were laughing together again, and slowly, in spurts, trust was building.

There were ripples in our sweet life, however. Out of nowhere, it seemed, Justin would hurl hostile accusations of infidelity at me. Those baffled me more than any of his other insults. Why did he keep coming back to the idea that I had cheated on him? Why did he always resort to the recrimination that I was a whore and a slut . . . and worse? Those monikers became branded on me, if not in a tangible way, at least in my mind.

I used to shrug off the idea that such a thing as verbal abuse existed. I mean, people can say whatever they want to you, but it's up to you to let it slide off your shoulders, right? They're just words.

Well, that whole saying about how sticks and stones can hurt but words don't is a big, fat lie.

It was at this point that I started to comprehend firsthand the depth, the enormity, the true scope of verbal abuse. Justin's words pierced a little deeper every time I heard his refrain: "You're a selfish b----! I can't believe I ever married you! You're nothing but a whore!" The words dug deep into my soul, penetrating my thoughts and deteriorating my self-image.

Who among us hasn't had something awful said to us or about us? Something that rattled us, that sunk its teeth in and kept gnawing at us? Now amplify that experience by a million when it's not a stranger. When the person you love and are supposed to be able to trust most beats you to an emotional pulp, the offense is infinitely more painful. And even worse, you eventually start to believe what that person says.

Words are powerful. Particularly when they come from someone we love.

Put simply, words are powerful. Particularly when they're coming from someone we love.

The terrifying thing about this cycle is the way the ugliness evolves. It transfers from the abuser's mind to the victim's own thinking. Eventually I didn't need Justin to say the words—I began to berate myself for being stupid or incapable. I doubted my abilities and intelligence because it was what I heard from him, and it became more and more difficult to distinguish his voice from mine. At one time in my life I'd had a pretty clear understanding of who I was. Now I couldn't begin to describe myself to someone else. The person I knew to be me was vanishing.

———•———

Two years into our marriage, there was a night of volatility I couldn't ignore.

Justin came home as I was getting ready to go to work at four o'clock in the morning—yes, 4:00 a.m. He was inebriated and started pushing me around, telling me how worthless I was.

"You never would have made it this far without me, Christi! The only reason you made it to Phoenix was because I brought you here. You're nothing but a whore! How could I have been dumb enough to marry you?"

Then he started spouting about buying a gun and not wanting to live. This wasn't the first time he'd said something like this. In Boise he'd mentioned getting a gun and had made flippant, drunken statements about how he didn't want to live. But this time felt different. Something about the way he said, "I don't want to go on," made me afraid that this might be more than mere talk.

I wondered how far he might really go.

When chaos and threats encircle you, it's not just your mind that starts reeling. Your body eventually starts to react to it too. That's exactly what happened to me as Justin stood over me screaming. I started trembling uncontrollably. My muscles tensed up, and my teeth clenched.

My body was telling me what I'd been ignoring for too long.

When Justin passed out, I called his parents.

"I can't take it anymore," I told them. "I really think you should be here for him because I'm ready to leave." I said it firmly but with a hint of desperation. I think his mother could hear the urgency and pleading in my voice.

By midafternoon his father was walking off a plane at Phoenix Sky Harbor International Airport. I picked him up and we went to dinner, where I filled him in on what had been going on for the past two years.

I'd made a couple of other phone calls that day—one to a friend who said she had a truck and could help me move if need be, and one to find an available apartment that I could move into immediately.

For the first time, the possibility of leaving Justin was actually in motion. If this life wasn't going to change, I was going to change things myself—for my own sake.

As I talked to Justin's dad, I realized he hadn't been completely oblivious. He had an inkling that Justin and I were having some issues, but I don't think he knew they'd escalated to this point.

Justin's parents had embraced me as their daughter-in-law from the beginning. As soon as we announced our engagement, his mom, Anna, arranged two wedding showers so I could get to know their extended family and friends. She was a woman of style, and we shopped together, shared recipes, and swapped home decor ideas. And I loved the way his dad, Mark, chuckled whenever he called and heard my enthusiastic "Helloooo, Dad!" He'd respond in kind with a "Helloooo, Christi!" I could practically hear him smiling through the phone.

I was—and still am—grateful to Justin's parents for all they did for us. They pulled out all the stops to come to our rescue as a couple and to Justin as their son. I loved them dearly, and they helped sustain me during that time.

Late that night as I lay in bed, I heard Justin turn the key of the front door and walk in. Then I heard his father say, "Hello, Justin." His voice was solid and determined. This was no "Hey, I'm here! How've you been?"

I can't imagine what went through Justin's head when he saw his father sitting on the couch, waiting for him.

"What are you doing here?" I heard Justin ask. I could hear the fear in his voice. At that moment he reverted back to a little boy who had just gotten caught doing something he wasn't supposed to do. He knew he was busted.

"I'm here to help you save your marriage because you're about to lose it," Mark said. "Now go to bed. We'll talk tomorrow."

I just lay there in bed, my eyes closed and my body tense.

What was Justin going to do? Would he walk in and let me have it? How mad would he be that I'd called in the troops—a solid force all wrapped up in the form of his father?

But Justin walked into our room, crawled into bed, and put his arm around me.

It was sweet and loving. And totally unexpected. It said to me that he really wanted to work this out.

I lay there with my eyes closed but wide awake. For the first time in a long time, I had hope.

———•———

I got up the next morning and went to work, giving Justin and his dad some privacy. I don't know what Mark said to Justin or what Justin revealed to his father over the next few days. But I do know that had it not been for his parents' intervention, it would have ended there.

When Mark and I were alone at dinner the night before he flew home, he said something that stuck with me. "Christi," he said, "alcoholism is a disease. It's like cancer. You can't just say, 'I don't want this, so I'm not going to have that drink.' It's not that easy. You can't just decide to control it. Not without help."

In other words, Justin was sick. When he lashed out at me, it wasn't necessarily because he believed all those vulgarities he spewed but because he had a disease that overtook him. That didn't make it okay, mind you, and it didn't mean Justin wasn't responsible for his actions. But it did give me more perspective to try to understand where he was coming from.

One thing I was starting to understand was that we needed to get Justin help . . . and he had to be willing to accept it.

Mark's words echoed in my head over the next several weeks. As I started to absorb the gravity of this disease and what it was doing to Justin and to our marriage, I got my first true taste of hopelessness. And apparently, I couldn't conceal it.

My boss, O'Neill, called me into his office one day.

"How are you doing?" he asked.

"What do you mean?" I questioned. I wondered silently, *Did I screw up a story?* I hadn't been late to anything; I hadn't missed a deadline. I was pretty sure I hadn't said anything during our shows that would prompt the FCC to haul me off the set.

It turned out O'Neill was a pretty observant guy. "You haven't been yourself lately," he said. "People come to expect a certain demeanor from you because, you know, you're a happy person. That hasn't really been you lately. There are some people in the newsroom who are concerned for you right now, and I wanted to know if there's anything I can do."

Busted!

I could no longer hide this problem from other people. Which meant I could no longer hide it from myself, either.

So right there in my boss's office, I let it out. I explained that I was going through some issues at home, and I hadn't realized they'd been consuming me so noticeably.

O'Neill responded immediately with his support. "If you're not happy at home, you're not going to be happy at work, and vice versa. You need to take care of yourself. Just let me know what you need from us."

I drove home that night trying again to keep it all inside. I was determined to remain stoic. Emotionless. Almost robotic.

Mark's words were still ringing in my ear: "This is a disease. It's like cancer. You can't decide not to have it."

I walked up the steps to our apartment, turned the key, and walked in. As I shut the door behind me, I literally collapsed, bawling.

That's the picture of hopelessness: a grown woman, on her knees, gasping for breath between each sob. Yeah. Not a pretty picture.

It finally sank in that I had absolutely no control over this situation. Every time Justin drank, it wasn't an indication that he didn't love me enough to stop. It wasn't about me—it wasn't about us at all. It was about him.

I'd tried every tactic known to humankind, and I couldn't make this situation better. I could beg Justin to stop drinking, I could threaten to leave, I could plead with him to accept my love and let me help him, but until *he* made the decision to tackle this head-on, nothing I could do would work.

I don't know how long I sat there on the floor crying. I felt helpless . . . and utterly alone. I might as well have been in the middle of the ocean in a small dinghy, just waiting to die.

———•———

One ray of hope had emerged from Mark's visit, and I clung to it like a life buoy. Justin had agreed to go to counseling with me.

This felt like a crucial step for us to take if we were ever going to break the cycle we were in. I desperately needed Justin to absorb the enormity of what his drinking was doing to me—and to us. I needed him to be accountable for his actions. The point wasn't to punish him but to help him realize how the alcohol was shredding our relationship to pieces. I felt like he was clueless about how serious this issue really was.

The counseling wasn't just for him, either. I had to deal with problems that were just as debilitating to our marriage as his were. For one thing, I needed help learning how to deal with the resentment I'd held in for so long. I was angry that he'd treated me like this for the past two years. Angry that I'd let it happen. Angry that I hadn't stood my ground and insisted that he deal with it sooner.

Another issue that often came up between Justin and me was that I didn't always let him in emotionally. Honestly, I didn't know how to let my guard down with him anymore. After so many verbal beatings, I felt emotionally pulverized, and I'd built up this iron fortress to guard myself against his next drunken tirade.

I began to envision alcoholism as the body of an octopus, with the tentacles representing all the issues that stem from it. Deceit, anger, verbal abuse, deflection, humiliation. These weren't things we could remotely deal with on our own.

Clearly, there was work to be done on both of our parts. And for once, we both took our parts seriously.

———•———

Our counselor reminded me of a younger, hipper Robin Williams (not that Robin Williams isn't hip). He had a freeing sense of humor that could break the tension and ease us into a comfortable place when things started to get too acrimonious.

A girlfriend had told me about Dr. Anderson, recommending him as a solid Christian counselor. I wasn't sure how Justin would react to that, as he wasn't a man of faith, but thank goodness, he liked him too.

It was important to me to get guidance from someone of faith. God was the one I'd turned to all my life whenever trouble struck, even though I was becoming woefully aware of how often I questioned Him myself. I believed in God, certainly. Believing He'd save me from whatever pit I was in was another part of faith altogether. I'd faced Melissa being murdered, P.A. killing himself, my marriage crumbling to pieces, and far too many tragedies among my friends to count. But at the end of the day, God was still my go-to guy.

Justin didn't grow up that way, though. While he wasn't someone who frequented church or seemed to follow any religious tenets, he didn't completely shut the door to the idea of faith and God. He went to church with me a couple of times, and he accepted that faith was a big part of my life—he just didn't necessarily partake in it himself. And if he had a relationship with God, well, he certainly never shared it with me.

Dr. Anderson gave us tests to evaluate our mental and emotional states. Two certainties came out of those tests. Number one, Justin had real alcohol issues. Number two, I was sinking into depression. Gee, ya think?

We both knew it was going to be hard for Justin to face his demons. According to Dr. Anderson, there were some wars he needed to win, and those would take place on two battlefields.

For one thing, he was going to have to come to terms with his alcohol issues and all the damage alcohol had done to him and to our relationship.

On another field, he had to start playing his life game differently from here on out. That meant a life without alcohol, which would require him to form new habits, make new strategies, and break old patterns. This alcohol-free life had a whole new set of rules to play by. He had to learn to recognize his own capabilities and identify situations that were just too tempting for him. And in those moments when temptation found him, he'd have to find the strength to walk away. I knew that was going to be torture for him.

My assignment, for starters, was to find a way to let go of the past and live in the here and now. I couldn't erase the abuse that had occurred, but I needed to learn how to dismantle it and put it behind me. I needed to forgive and move on.

I couldn't erase the abuse that had occurred, but I needed to learn how to dismantle it and put it behind me. I needed to forgive and move on.

I was proud of Justin as I watched him making a true effort. Even though he still came home after I was in bed, he was, indeed, coming home more often than he went out with the crew. He was pouring more of his energy into work, and during his free time he was reading and writing—even talking about writing a fiction book. It was clearly a struggle, but he was trying.

I ached for him, wishing I could do more to help. I saw that he yearned to be free from alcoholism. I clung to the hope that his drive would suit him as well in this battle as it had in professional settings. That ambition, that will to conquer, was one of the things I loved about him. It would be just what he needed to whip this liquid demon into submission.

As for me, I felt the relief of having someone I could finally vent to without fear of judgment. I desperately wanted to stay true to who I really was while at the same time helping Justin and being the person he needed. I was grateful to have Dr. Anderson to help me find that balance.

We both had a long way to go, but we knew what we needed to do to get there. One small step at a time.

The author Beth Moore writes, "God will hold each person accountable. The question is whether we will do our job."

I not only wanted to do my job, but I also wanted to do it well and fully.

So Justin faced his alcoholism; I faced my resentment. And things got better. In fact, they got really good.

For about a year.

KEEP THE FAITH

HAVE YOU EVER looked back at a situation and realized you should have seen it coming? Something was about to implode, and on some level, you sensed it? In the days or months leading up to the finale, there was a shadow that followed you everywhere—a cloud of sorts that blanketed your soul. And even though you weren't sure what it was or why it was there, you knew something was happening. Something was changing.

That's what happened to me.

In the months before my cloud burst into a full-fledged storm, I was happily living in denial. In the nine or ten months since we'd started counseling, Justin and I had seemed to swing past our, well, past. He wasn't drinking, that I knew of. He wasn't quite as edgy. I could see him holding his tongue when he wanted to rail. He'd bite his lip or shake his head instead of blowing up. Sometimes he'd sit and listen to me without jumping in to convince me to see something his way.

I even overheard him bragging about me a few times, about the painting I was doing at home. And I noticed how proud he was standing on the sideline when I sang the national anthem at the Diamondbacks games. He was proud of me. He was making time for me. I was flooded by the warmth of that feeling—the memory of what it was like to have value in the eyes of the one you love.

That's how it was for us for a while. We got our happiness back, our laughter back. We got our trust back—or at least some of it. Enough to sustain us for almost a year.

But slowly, an uneasiness began percolating under the surface of my faux contentment.

One thing that should have served as a warning sign was that, against my better judgment, we stopped going to counseling. After just a few months of seeing Dr. Anderson, things started evening out—the emotional roller coaster slowed down a bit, and the hills were less bumpy. So it felt safer to let go a little. And that's what I did. At first I resisted when Justin said he wanted to halt our counseling sessions. But eventually I gave in—partly out of fear and partly because I didn't want to seem like I was dismissing the progress he'd made. I didn't want him to think I didn't believe he could do this on his own.

Another warning bell for me was an e-mail I received from my dear friend Colleen, who had just visited from Ohio. She and I had breakfast together, and seeing her was a striking reminder of what it was like to feel accepted and secure. When she e-mailed me after our get-together, her words were medicine on emotional wounds I'd been trying to ignore.

Christi,

Although you're reporting current happiness, I worry about you and how it seems you've had some very lonely/sad times over the past couple of years. But you can always count on me. Ya know what, sometimes things just don't happen as we expect them to. I have to tell you how much respect I have for you, C. The fact that you are going to do whatever it takes, that you're fighting to keep this together, is a sign of your grace and strength. God is in control, as we both know, and He will never let us down. I'm so grateful to have met you on this journey. Be good to you.

I sat at my desk just staring at her message. It pierced me. Those words *grace* and *respect*—I just couldn't imagine them next to my name anymore. To hear that someone saw me in that light, to hear that someone was grateful to know me—it was shocking. And healing. For the first time in a long time, I felt needed. I felt humbled. And I felt loved.

As I go back now and read my journals from that time, I see that the pages are filled with the gratefulness I felt. I was thankful for my family, for my job, for Justin's family, and even for Justin . . . particularly on the good days. But being grateful for how God might be working through *me*? That was a foreign concept. After being emotionally trampled for so long, it's hard to see yourself as more than what your husband says you are.

About a month later I was on vacation back home and had gone for a walk in the summer sunshine with Gram. My dear Gram. She was in her eighties and still as quick as a whip. Gram and I were really close not only because I was named after her but because she also took care of me when I was little while my parents worked. She was available to everyone—anytime, anywhere. She attended every one of my basketball games, cheerleading competitions, school plays, and choir productions.

And she had a will of steel. My grandfather died when I was four, so the clearest image I have of Gram is a woman who wasn't afraid to be alone. That woman would not bend if she had her mind made up. Feisty? Yes, indeed.

That afternoon she and I talked about our family, my work, her volunteering at church and the hospital. Then my marriage came up. I finally confided in her some of the things Justin and I had been struggling with in the last few years—leaving out the gory details, of course.

I knew she had some firsthand knowledge about gory details herself. My grandfather, too, was an alcoholic.

Grandpa was a pilot in World War II, and after he came home, he never spoke about what he'd witnessed. I know he lost friends in the war and probably saw things I can't even fathom, nor would I want to. All those terrible images that were burned into his mind from the war—that's what Gram believes drove him to the bottle.

Gram turned to me. "Christi, your grandpa and I had a beautiful twenty-four-year marriage!" She glowed as she said it.

The thing is, they were married for thirty-two years. Apparently the last eight were pretty awful. "That's when the alcohol stole him from me," she said. She told me he became someone she didn't recognize—someone very mean—when he drank.

Gram told me that for years she'd prayed, asking God what she should do. She always heard Him say, "Not yet. Stay." Then finally one day she sensed that the answer had changed: "Now. Go."

It was summertime, and as usual she left for the cottage they always rented by the lake. But that summer was not like summers past. She had just prepared the paperwork for a formal separation. Knowing how much Gram loved Grandpa, I imagine that had to be the most difficult move of her life. Then she got the call. Grandpa was dead. He'd died at home, but that's about all I know. But I've been told the alcohol finally killed him.

I admired Gram for being able to look back and focus on the sweet memories and wonderful times in her marriage, despite all that had happened. I assured her that things were better on my end. She squeezed my hand and smiled. "I hope so."

I have no doubt Gram's prayers for me changed that day. We now shared a common experience—one neither of us would have chosen. I can only guess that her prayer for guidance and security for me took center stage as she knelt before God on my behalf.

I have been blessed to have a family that prays for each other. They've shown me that God honors prayer. That when we lift our voices to Him, even if it's to complain or plead or tell Him we're mad at Him, He listens. He understands. And He is willing to start the healing process as soon as we open our hearts and give Him the green light to do it.

I had no idea that day how desperately I would need those prayers—and an open heart—in the weeks ahead.

———•———

It was the beginning of autumn, and I was flying to Chicago for our second annual "spa getaway" with my girlfriend Rachel. As the plane lifted off, my anxiety rose too. While on the surface things had been quieter at home lately, there were rumblings I could no longer ignore.

I noticed Justin had started going out more often after work again. When I confronted him about it, he just made excuses. We were on separate shifts, which meant I was asleep by the time he got home. So it became my fault that he didn't come home right away. "Well, you're already in bed, so what am I going to come home to?" he'd argue.

Several weeks before my Chicago trip, I heard him walk into the apartment with a couple of people around one in the morning. One of those voices belonged to a woman. I knew her—it was one of his coworkers. A chilling thought ran down my spine. *What if he's cheating on me?*

I wasn't blind to the signs. We rarely are. We just choose to ignore them.

I remember standing looking in the bathroom mirror the next morning wondering whether I should investigate . . . and being scared to do it. Afraid of what I might discover he'd been up to in those wee hours when I was home alone. The mere thought of him with another woman made me shiver.

But as I looked at my reflection in the mirror, I said to myself, *That's nuts, Christi. He wouldn't be fool enough to bring her back to our place. He wouldn't be that stupid or that bold.* But I couldn't help but wonder what was going on while I was at home in bed.

I wasn't blind to the signs. We rarely are. We just choose to ignore them.

To make matters worse, a couple of people had approached me individually in the past few weeks and confided that they'd seen Justin out with a drink in hand. Each time I confronted him about it, he accused me of not trusting him and claimed he'd been drinking nonalcoholic beer. Arguing with him got me nowhere, and since I hadn't seen it firsthand, I didn't feel like I had enough evidence to nail him on it. Two things I knew: (1) he wasn't telling me everything. And (2) I was losing the energy to keep fighting.

When you hammer and claw at a wall of bricks, trying valiantly to break it down but merely chipping away at the surface, eventually your muscles start to sputter and ache. Your fingertips get raw. Exhaustion bleeds from your bones to your soul, and you finally drop the hammer. How much more can you give before you collapse?

The moment I stepped off the plane into the terminal at Midway Airport, I had one of those jolts of awareness that shoots through your entire body. I felt an unexpected rush of freedom, and with it came a realization: I wanted to rip up my return ticket. I did not want to go back.

The fragrant autumn air was refreshing for this Midwestern girl's heart. It brought back fond memories of football games, vibrant leaves, and pumpkin carving. The air was crisp and cool, and the rustling trees sounded like a symphony in the breeze. But there was something deeper happening than just the weather. Being here took me back to where I'd come from and who I was. I was finally remembering the alive Christi—the person God made me to be. This was a feeling I hadn't been in touch with in years.

Rachel and her husband, Steve, greeted me with such warmth. They welcomed me into their home as if the room they'd prepared had been waiting for me all along. Over the next few days Rachel and I explored the city. We ate at great restaurants, got massages and spa treatments, shopped until we couldn't carry even one more bag, and guffawed the entire time, our laughter ringing in harmony with the whirling and bustling of the city.

By the second night of my visit, I became acutely aware of a shift in me. We all know when this happens—we just don't always embrace it. Sometimes we even fight it because we know it means change, and change is scary.

Rachel and I were sitting by the fire that night as the steady melody of raindrops fell outside the window. Suddenly it hit me that the shift in me was contentment. After four years of feeling unsafe, I was finally able to breathe easy. To laugh honestly. To sit peacefully. To be myself—not the suspicious, tense version of me I'd become in the past couple of years. For the first time in a long time, I felt secure.

Encased in the warmth of Rachel's apartment, I felt not just physical safety but emotional safety. I felt taken care of, valued. I sensed that these friends wanted me there and appreciated my company. And because of all that, I felt free. Free to be who I was without fear of ridicule or judgment, without fear of being demeaned or hurt. I could laugh as loudly as I wanted to, and no one would shoot me a glaring look. I could tell a story without having someone roll his eyes; I could make a comment without anyone shaking his head at me. And once I'd tasted that freedom again—the freedom to be myself—I realized it was torturous to consider returning to a person or a life that paralyzed me.

I just couldn't go back to the way things were in Phoenix. Having experienced walking on a firm foundation in the Midwest, I physically ached when I thought of returning to the floor of eggshells I'd tiptoed around each day back in the desert.

The last day of my visit I called my dad to wish him a happy birthday. Hearing him sound so happy to talk to me made my heart skip a beat. When I hung up, I felt the tears coming.

"What's wrong?" Rachel asked.

I shook my head. "I don't know."

I couldn't put my finger on it at first, but gradually things started getting clearer.

"I feel so free when I'm here with you and when I talk to my dad. Justin has never really tried to be part of my family. He doesn't really like my dad, and that hurts so much. I sometimes feel like I have to choose."

"Between Justin and your dad?" Rachel asked.

"Yeah. No one has ever said it out loud, but I feel so disconnected from my family when I'm with Justin. If I had made that phone call from home, I know Justin wouldn't have gotten on the phone to wish Dad happy birthday. He'd just make up an excuse not to talk to him, like he always does."

"Why don't we go for a walk and talk?" Rachel suggested.

So we put on our workout clothes and took a long, brisk walk by the lake. When we got to some picnic tables, we sat down. That's when I finally said it. It practically fell out of my mouth without my even thinking about it.

"This marriage I'm in will not last forever."

Rachel just looked at me, curious but not shocked.

I took a breath and continued. "Something is going to have to change. It's just a matter of my getting the courage to do something about it."

There! I'd said it.

It was the first time I'd made a statement like that. Not just out loud, but even to myself. I'd often had hypothetical thoughts:

What if this marriage doesn't last? *What if* I have to leave? *What if* he doesn't stop drinking or lying or being mean? But now, to be so unequivocal about it—well, I startled myself.

I don't even remember what Rachel said in response. I'm sure she expressed her support and said that she would always be there for me and so would my family. My mind was still whirling at the truth I'd just spoken out loud.

God never leaves us broken on the floor without extending His hand to lift us up again.

Rachel and I walked home slowly as she asked questions and I opened up about this faux life I'd been living—how I'd been feigning happiness and confidence not only to fool everyone else, but perhaps even more so, to convince myself.

Here's what I learned the hard way: we can lie to ourselves only so long before we either break down or wake up. Sometimes we do both. We just need to have faith that the wake-up call is ready for us on the other side of the meltdown. God never leaves us broken on the floor without extending His hand to lift us up again.

As I got ready for bed that evening, I couldn't help but wish— from somewhere so deep in my soul it hurt—that I could just stay in Chicago. I dreamed of getting a job here, finding a little place of my own, even if it was the size of a closet, and starting over. I was desperate to feel this kind of freedom every day, to find hope again. The last four years my life had revolved around keeping the peace, trying to make Justin happy, overcoming turmoil. I believed that God intended more for my life. Could I find the courage to embrace it?

On that final evening of my trip, I looked in the mirror and saw someone I hadn't seen in years.

I saw me.

My hazel eyes were clear again. I saw a girl who had dreams. Who had hope. Who was revived and reenergized.

And I sobbed.

I sobbed because I missed that person, and I wasn't sure if she'd stick around. I sobbed because I knew in the morning I was getting on a plane to go back to a life that stifled me—a life that scared me.

How could I possibly go back?

As I stared at myself through tear-filled eyes, makeup smearing down my face, my denial finally evaporated. Or more accurately, it blew up in my face.

In the past few days I'd remembered my roots, and the process revealed to me something terrifying: the pre-Justin Christi was not the same person as the post-Justin Christi. Sure, there were certain elements of the new me that resembled the old. But I wanted some of those pieces back: the living-life-out-loud Christi. The Christi who believed in faith. The Christi who looked for the goodness of people. The Christi who wanted to live a purposeful existence.

Pastor Miller's words on our wedding day, "Remember your roots," were echoing in my mind as I lay my head on the pillow that night. I had remembered what it felt like to just be me. No excuses or apologies necessary. No shields of protection up to deflect the criticisms I'd become accustomed to. I felt like I was standing on solid ground for the first time in years.

The problem was, that solid ground was about to get very shaky.

The next morning in the cab, I cried all the way to the airport as I talked to Rachel on the phone. The cabbie had to think I was a total whack job! I can imagine him getting on his phone as soon as I set foot on the curb, saying, "You won't believe what I just had to listen to!"

I told Rachel everything—that I didn't want to go back, that for the first time I truly didn't know what was going to happen in my marriage. I didn't know if I could stay with Justin.

I felt like I had to force myself to get on the plane—to coax myself to take one step, then another, then another until I made it to my seat. I just wanted to turn around and run back to Rachel's.

My head was spinning the whole flight home. Two things had become clear to me on this trip: (1) I had discovered myself again. I'd regained the freedom to be myself without fear. And (2) I knew for the first time that I did not want to stay in this marriage. Not the way it was.

That realization broke my heart. I couldn't even comprehend hurting Justin like that because I loved him. I wanted him to be happy. But I couldn't keep holding my misery inside.

That's what happens when we lose ourselves, for whatever reason—whether it's money, fame, love, jealousy, or pride. If those things make us something we're not, if they twist our core beings into some warped versions of ourselves, we'll feel it. Eventually our souls will recognize what's happening and ache for our real selves to come back.

We're not primarily skeletons walking around armed with skin. We're souls armed with faith. With light. With love. And the moment we let something or someone steal our personhood, our spirits start fighting to bring us back. That's why when something is amiss, we walk around feeling anxious and empty. If we're not where we belong, on some internal level we feel it.

We are not just a collection of all the mistakes we've made, the choices we've botched, the consequences we've miscalculated. First and foremost, we're children of God, and that is enough. He has created us to shine. It's just that there's part of us that's afraid of that light.

On the flight home, I prayed, "God, give me the strength to know what to do. I can't do this alone. I don't even know what I'm supposed to do anymore. Do I stay? Do I go? Give me some guidance!"

I was too scared to admit it, but what I was really saying was, "How do I go? How do I leave him?" I looked out the window at the mountains and the clouds, and I heard a voice, as clear as if it were coming from the person in the seat next to me: "Christi, I love you as far as you can see . . . and then some."

Our pain tells us we're not okay as we are. God tells us otherwise.

It was a message I desperately needed to hear. I had to know that I wasn't alone. It wasn't a direct answer about what to do next, but it did give me comfort. I sat back and exhaled.

My mind replayed the trip over and over. Being with these people showed me that it is truly a gift from God to be accepted for who we are—imperfect parts and all. Our pain tells us we're not okay as we are. God tells us otherwise. My problem was that I hadn't listened to Him enough in the last few years. I'd been too preoccupied waking up each morning steeling myself for the next blowup.

I'm not perfect, but God doesn't expect me to be. I just have to be real. My challenge now was to keep hold of that realness, despite that battle on the horizon.

CHAPTER 7

REFUSE TO PLAY SMALL

I WALKED IN the door of our apartment and collapsed into a chair. My head hurt, my eyes burned, and I was exhausted. I looked around at this place I called home. It was peaceful . . . when I was there alone.

I hadn't realized how mind numbing it had become to walk around on a minefield whenever Justin was around, knowing it could explode with any wrong step I made. I had absorbed this as a lifestyle—it was just how I made it through each day.

But now, having lived four days free of these emotional confines, I knew I couldn't simply go back to living a myopic life. Things didn't look the same to me anymore.

I called my mom, telling her how rejuvenating Chicago was, and I spilled everything. My suspicions that Justin was drinking and lying to me again. How I felt like I'd found myself again, and how I wasn't sure I could go on like this. How I knew something had to change if we were going to work this out.

God bless my mom. I've always said she has a private phone line straight to Him. She's a prayer warrior, and I knew she would start praying for me the moment we hung up the phone. She told me she knew Justin loved me very much but if he wasn't willing to face his alcohol issues, then yes, I might have to leave. In the four years we'd been married, that was the first time she'd ever said anything like that to me.

I got off the phone and wrapped my fingers together, praying for guidance and wisdom and strength. And the strangest thing happened—I could feel myself letting go of "control." My angst about what to do next was lifting. I sensed that God was telling me that my job right now was to wait. And that's what I did.

What happened next only convinced me that God had His hands all over this situation. He'd heard my prayer.

The next day I ran into a friend of ours who was somewhat aware of our struggles. She told me that while I was gone, she had seen Justin drinking. I could tell she was treading lightly because she knew this was a delicate situation, but I was grateful for her honesty and compassion. She wasn't trying to bust him—she simply could see that something wasn't lining up, and she wanted to help me.

I asked Justin about it later that night. Sure enough, I got the same old spiel.

"Come on, Christi! Did she look at the bottle? Did she notice it was nonalcoholic? Did you ever stop to think what it's like for me to be out there and not drink when everyone else is? And to have them wonder why I'm not drinking? Have you ever thought about how that makes me feel?"

I couldn't help but think, *Really? What are we, in junior high? You're going to blame this on peer pressure?* But I didn't say it out loud. He was already getting riled up. That old fear had come back to me in full force. But things felt different this time. I felt stronger, and I knew for certain that something in this big picture just wasn't right.

But once again, I couldn't prove anything. Justin knew how to twist the story enough to bring a shadow of doubt to the situation. I hadn't been there. Was it O'Doul's? I couldn't prove it wasn't.

A few days later I found myself faced with another cause for suspicion. I opened the credit card bill and saw a charge I didn't know about. It was for two hundred dollars—from a bar. I asked Justin about it, and the way he responded was just as disturbing as the charge itself.

When I first confronted him, he told me it was an error on the part of the bar—that it should have been twenty dollars, and they'd obviously made a mistake. The next day I brought it up again, and his argument evolved into, "Oh, it was just a lot of food." And finally, when I wouldn't let it go, he said, "I bought the food and drinks for everyone else . . . but I didn't drink at all!"

Three times I gave him a chance to come clean with me. And three times he came up with a faux story. With each lie, I felt my footing slipping away. He grew more volatile every time we talked about it, until I finally just shut down.

With each passing day, the freedom I'd felt in Chicago started disintegrating. And brick by brick, that wall I'd been building around myself was cementing itself in place. Pretty soon the wall wouldn't let anything in at all. No lies. No hope. No joy. No love.

My only outlet was waking up at five every morning and

running. It was September in Phoenix, which meant triple-digit temperatures, so I had to run before the sun came up. A far cry from the crisp autumn air I'd left in Chicago. As I ran, I listened to a tape my friend Colleen had sent me with music and insights from several authors. I clung to one song in particular by Pam Thum: "Life Is Hard (God Is Good)." It was a powerful reminder that even when I felt battered and close to defeat, I could still cling to the hope that regardless of my circumstances, God had my back.

No one can take a part of you unless you let them.

There was also a quote on the tape that God used to get my attention. When I heard these words by Marianne Williamson, the rhythmic pounding of my feet came to an abrupt halt.

"Our deepest fear is not that we are inadequate. Our deepest fear is that we are powerful beyond measure. It is our light, not our darkness, that most frightens us. We ask ourselves, 'Who am I to be brilliant, gorgeous, talented, fabulous?' Actually, who are you not to be? You are a child of God. Your playing small does not serve the world."

I stood there in the middle of the sidewalk, trying to catch my breath and process these words.

It had been a lifetime since I viewed myself as anything close to brilliant, talented, or fabulous. Now, *inadequate*, on the other hand—that was something I could relate to. After four years of listening to someone belittle, accuse, and abuse me, I couldn't imagine seeing myself as anything other than small. Somehow Justin's words had overtaken my own.

Here's what I've learned to be true: no one can take a part of you unless you let them. They can try. They can even physically

86

take something from you. But your self-worth, your self-esteem, your soul—no one can swipe those from you unless you allow them to. Yes, I'd been hiding God's light in me out of fear that Justin would attack it if I let it loose. And at this point, I wasn't even sure if I had any light left.

The dry desert air seeped into my nose as I breathed in and out, in and out. I stood there wondering, *Who am I? What do I want? Who do I want to be?*

I hadn't explored such thoughts in a long time. As I walked home, pondering those questions, what blared in my mind was how short I'd fallen in the last few years. But more than that, I forced myself to explore what was causing these shortcomings.

One thing that became clear was that I wasn't concentrating on work like I wanted to. I didn't read as much as I used to, and I was no longer jumping full force into my job. Suddenly it dawned on me that I'd been sabotaging myself. I was afraid to excel at work because I knew Justin would just have something to say about it. I never knew when he'd lay into me again with demeaning comments about my never making it this far without him. But regardless of Justin's role in this, I had to take ownership of the fact that I was choosing to live a small life. Maybe I was choosing out of fear, but it was still my choice—and I couldn't blame that on Justin.

My second revelation was that I'd lost the tight connection to my family that had always been so important to me. I didn't go home to Ohio as often as I would have liked because Justin wasn't a fan of my father, which baffled everyone I knew. My father is dearly loved and respected—and for good reason. He's a man of incredible compassion, integrity, and strength. My folks were adoptive parents of sorts to some of my friends, and even when I was away at college, they would sometimes pop in just to see my mom and dad. But in the four years we'd been married, Justin and I had only gone to my parents' house twice—once when we stopped through on our way to Justin's brother's wedding, and once for Christmas. Justin didn't like going there—he said there was nothing to do. I guess it just didn't seem worth the battle to me to convince Justin to go home with me. Looking back, I saw now that although Justin certainly made it difficult, I was still responsible for caving on that front.

The third thing I admitted to myself was that I didn't volunteer as much as I wanted to. Why? Again, it just didn't feel like it was worth the battle. For some time I'd wanted to find a place to volunteer my time, but whenever I brought it up with Justin, he shot down the idea. Just a few months earlier I'd told Justin I wanted to start volunteering with a children's charity. He shot back, "Are you kidding? Why would you do that? It'll only cut into our time together!"

In that moment of honesty as I walked home, I realized I had been so consumed with the turmoil at home and making sure Justin was okay that I'd let my dreams for myself disintegrate. I'd compromised so much of my life just to try to make Justin happy. And as long as I'm being honest, let's just lay it out there: this wasn't done strictly out of the goodness of my heart. The truth is, I knew that if Justin was happy, then life was pretty peaceful. And most days I was just shooting for peace.

You know you're in a sad state when you've given someone that kind of power over your life. And for me it was all so gradual that by the time I realized what was happening, it felt like things were too far gone to be fixed.

I stood in the parking lot of our apartment building as the sun began to rise. Instead of going inside, I sat on the step watching the brilliant golden hues paint the desert sky. Even as I soaked in the beauty, I couldn't ignore the realization that in my attempt to keep the peace, I had indeed been playing small.

The churning in my gut told me how dangerous this tactic would be over the long haul. I was learning that when you play small—when you bury your true feelings and aspirations—you start to morph into a zombie. And that's not the life God intended for us. But it was certainly what I'd become. Walking comatose.

We sometimes fool ourselves into thinking that being numb is a show of strength. But in reality it's a defense mechanism. We figure if we don't allow anything or anyone in, then we can't be hurt, right? But as I watched the warm yellow beams of light streaking into the sky, I realized that if we shut ourselves off, we also can't know joy. Or peace. Or purpose.

Suddenly, as the new day was breaking, I started to feel something. I wasn't sure exactly what it was, but it felt like a little glimmer of hope. No bigger than a grain of sand, maybe, but it was there nonetheless. Hope that God had put me on this earth for something more than this. Hope that I was born to live an abundant life—a life of authenticity.

If we shut ourselves off, we also can't know joy. Or peace. Or purpose.

For the next few days I ruminated over this idea of who I really was and what God might want me to do with my life. At home alone one night, sitting on the floor after a tough workout, I breathed deeply and lay on my back, relaxing my muscles and my mind. My thoughts wandered to all that I'd been exploring about myself and God the last few days. I thought back to when I was a teenager and all the things I'd dreamed for my life.

I wanted to sing. I wanted to tell stories. I wanted to make enough money to support myself. I wanted to be a mom and a wife who was passionately in love with her husband.

Sure, as a journalist I got to tell people's stories, and I'd had opportunities to sing on several occasions. I made enough money to take care of myself. But the rest—the emotional connections and family relationships—was nothing more than a fuzzy dream. I still longed to be a mom, but I couldn't imagine bringing a child into this chaos. I ached at the realization that I was a woman who was no longer in love with my husband. And worst of all, the real me was dying each day I stayed in this marriage. I knew I wasn't serving my purpose by being here.

Bam! There it was—a one-liner that smacked my soul awake. It was like a flashing sign proclaiming the words that would start my journey back to myself: *You aren't serving God by being in this marriage.*

God may put us in uncomfortable positions sometimes. But His purpose in those times is for us to grow, not for us to fail.

Now, serving God doesn't mean you have to sell all your possessions, leave everyone you love, and proclaim His name in a developing country, so don't panic. I think there's a real misconception out there about what it means to serve God. Yes, He might call some people to serve Him in a dramatic way overseas, but for others it's more about conscious daily choices in the midst of ordinary life.

I believe serving God means being true to who He made you to be. It means allowing yourself to feel and be cognizant of the God-given desires stirring inside you. He isn't going to call you to be a doctor if the sight of blood makes you queasy. He isn't going to ask you to step onto a stage and sing if you're tone deaf and prone to stage fright. It's true that God may put us in uncomfortable positions sometimes. But His purpose in those times is for us to grow, not for us to fail.

I knew unequivocally that I wasn't being all He wanted me to be, because I wasn't serving Him. I was serving myself—in a dangerous way. I was serving myself fear on a silver platter. Every day.

In this marriage I had been feasting on fear—fear of speaking my mind, fear of fighting for what I needed, fear of standing up for what was right. That fear bled into every aspect of my life, and soon I was afraid to aspire. Afraid to let people in. Afraid to believe.

You know how that feels—being afraid to believe in anything that really matters. In God. In yourself. In other people. Because what if we believe . . . and the dream doesn't come true? What are we left with, aside from pulverized hope?

The realization that we're terrified to believe can come gradually, or it can hit us like the crack of a ball against a bat on a fast pitch—hard and deliberate.

For me it was kind of a trickle effect: slowly but surely, God was breaking through my lack of faith. I now had at least one solid answer to my questions about who I was and what I was meant to be. I might not have known what God had in store for my future, but I knew that this was *not* how He wanted me to live. That's not how He wants any of us to live.

Hear this loud and clear, my friends: you weren't put here to be abused. God's will isn't for us to wake up each day mired in fear, self-doubt, and condemnation. He wants us to see ourselves the way He sees us—wounded but worthy. To view ourselves and each other with forgiveness and grace. To trust and believe in Him despite where we've been, what we've done, or what someone told us we are.

In the past several years, I hadn't completely abandoned my faith, but I'd certainly given up the crux of it. Faith hadn't failed me—I'd failed it. My belief in certain core values was still there, but I'd tried to bury all that away somewhere. I suppose I saw truth as something I could wrap up in pretty paper and shove in the back of a closet somewhere. But at some point this animal was going to make itself known, and there would be no running from it. No matter how far I ran each morning or how fast my feet pounded the concrete, the truth was chasing me down. I could feel it catching up with me, and I knew it was getting closer to cornering me. I had no choice but to turn around and face it.

God never said the universe would cater to us. But He did promise that we'd never face any of it alone. And if God is for us, who can stop us?

I passionately believe that no matter who we are or where we come from, there's a truth we all share: each of us is meant for something wonderful. Sure, God never said it would be easy. He never promised us a cakewalk. He never said the universe would cater to us. But He did promise that we'd never face any of it alone. And if God is for us, who can stop us? If He's with us through all of it (and He is!), then doesn't He want us to have joy? Doesn't He want us to succeed?

He promises that if we keep searching for Him earnestly and believe in Him, we'll find peace, regardless of our circumstances. He longs for us to walk through the fire and come out on the other side stronger, more certain of His faithfulness, and more conscious of what we learned from being put through the heat. Maybe that's His method to this madness. Like sheets of glass, we are molded and shaped by the fire underneath us until we become more and more who we're meant to be.

As I lay on my back, thinking, a Bible verse started blinking in my head—one I hadn't read in a long time but one that was lodged deep in my soul. I ran to the bedroom and opened my Bible, searching for the verse I knew was highlighted somewhere in the New Testament. Sure enough, the words in yellow were just as poignant as I'd remembered:

We rejoice in the hope of the glory of God. Not only so, but we also rejoice in our sufferings, because we know that suffering produces perseverance; perseverance, character; and character, hope. And hope does not disappoint us, because God has poured out his love into our hearts by the Holy Spirit, whom he has given us.

ROMANS 5:2-5

I couldn't stop staring at that sentence: "Hope does not disappoint."

It was as though God was telling me, "Hang in there, girl! I've got your back. Just hold on a little longer!" I was finally starting to believe it was true: if God is for us—and He *is* for us—then who could possibly succeed against us?

As I was taking all this in, another thought occurred to me: this wasn't just about me. If this marriage wasn't making me who God wanted me to be, it probably wasn't what Justin needed either.

The truth may be painful, but it's also relentless. I had been praying for change—and perhaps what needed to change was my perspective. Perhaps if the issues weren't improving after all this time, maybe it was truth's way of forcing me to face the fact that there was a bigger change that needed to be made.

Wow. I needed some help to clear this up.

God said we can't do it alone—we need other people to come alongside us, especially as we face the fire. He has put people in our lives who can help us—and it was past time for me to employ one of them.

The next day I mustered enough courage to take step number one. Justin was standing in the bedroom when I walked in.

"I really want to go back and see Dr. Anderson," I said.

He looked at me, his face full of shock and annoyance. "Why?" he snapped.

"Come on, Justin. You know things aren't good right now. We need some help. I can't keep doing this. We're not communicating, I'm having some trust issues with you, and you're clearly not happy. We need this."

As much as I'd prepared myself for some push back from him, I wasn't prepared for the assault that came.

"It's your problem!" he shouted. He was going into tirade mode. "I'm not going back to that shrink! You know how much that's going to cost? If you want to go, then go ahead! It's not my problem—it's yours!"

What happened next horrified me. Before I could even respond, he did something I'd never seen before. He started hitting himself—and I don't mean just a slap on the wrist. He curled his hand into a fist and started punching himself in the face and on the head. I screamed for him to stop, and as I moved toward him to physically intervene, I froze. He was glaring at me with such fury that I couldn't take another step. My heart pounded in sheer terror.

We stood there looking at each other for a moment, and then I walked out. Not knowing where else to go, I went into the bathroom and shut the door. I looked at myself in the mirror and tried to comprehend what had just happened. *Is he okay?* I wondered. But I was too afraid to open the door. I started a bath, thinking that would at least buy me some time before I had to face him again. As I crawled into the hot water, I couldn't help but think, *What if he's hitting himself to stop from hitting me? And if that's the case, how long will it be before that actually happens?*

The next day I called Dr. Anderson.

CHAPTER 8

YOU ARE EQUIPPED WITH THE COURAGE YOU NEED

When we're feeling traumatized or confused or beat up, it's hard to hold on to perspective. That's why I'm a big supporter of counseling. Some problems are just too huge to handle alone.

I was grateful Dr. Anderson had counseled Justin and me two years before, because that meant he already had some background on our situation. He told me he was sorry for what we were going through and asked me a lot of questions about how I was doing and how Justin was doing. Even though I was at this session alone, I felt I was making some progress. I was able to talk freely, expressing my fears and doubts without criticism. I left Dr. Anderson's office feeling a little lighter, like a burden was slowly being lifted from me.

Still, after watching Justin punch himself and seeing his rage, I felt like I had no protection once I left Dr. Anderson's office. I had no way to gauge how far Justin might go if he heard something he didn't want to hear. So how did I tell him I needed to spend some time away from him—on my own?

Fortunately, I didn't even have to bring it up. Justin did that all on his own.

———•———

About a week after my first appointment with Dr. Anderson, everything blew up. Justin got mad about something—I'm not even sure what it was. I took Dr. Anderson's advice and got really honest with Justin. I asked him again about that two-hundred-dollar bar bill and told him straight out that I didn't believe he wasn't drinking. That's when he started railing on me, calling me names and spewing erratic, illogical excuses. At one point he looked straight at me and said, "Maybe we should just separate!"

I said nothing. I just sat there staring at him. One thing I'd learned from all the emotional abuse I'd taken was that once you say something, you can't take it back. Sure, you can apologize, but the sting of the words, the bite you feel in that moment, can't be erased. I knew firsthand the power of words, and I wanted to be very cautious with mine.

Justin yelled at me some more, and then he said, "Maybe the answer is that we just separate."

Again, I kept my mouth shut. I knew that once I agreed, there would be no going back. And I was afraid of how he'd react. Would he hurt himself? Would he hurt me? *Dear God, what should I do?*

After more of his tirade, he said it a third time: "I guess maybe we should just separate, Christi, because this isn't working!" Finally it dawned on me that this was it—this was the opening I'd been asking for. I felt like God was saying, "Hello! I'm giving you an out here, Christi! You don't even have to say the words—he has already said it. Trust Me in this."

Now, I don't know if God actually talks to us like that, but those are absolutely the words I sensed from Him. I suddenly felt emboldened. Courageous. Is it possible to be scared out of your mind and intrepid at the same time? Let me tell you—yes, it is.

So I took a deep breath, looked at Justin, and said, "I guess maybe we should." As soon as the words were out of my mouth, my muscles tensed. I guess I was subconsciously bracing for the attack.

Just as I suspected, the roof blew off our apartment. Justin was like a tornado, whirling back and forth from one end of the room to the other. He'd get right up in my face and then bolt from room to room screaming at me, hands flailing. Finally he went into the bedroom and packed a suitcase, calling me names the whole time. "You stupid b----! This is it! It's over. No separation. This is divorce!"

I sat on the couch, terrified to move. Tears were streaming down my face, and I was shaking uncontrollably. I could feel it coming now. The end. It was right there in front of me.

I wanted to be anywhere but in this moment. I wished I could either hit the rewind button and erase what was happening or push fast-forward and get to the other side of this as fast as I could. But I was stuck there, in the present.

Justin came into the living room and stood over me, waving his finger at me.

"This is divorce! There will be no separation! Do you really want me to walk out that door? Because once I do, I'm never coming back! You're such a selfish b----. I never want to see you again!"

He walked into the bathroom, and a split second later he walked back out—completely calm. He sat in the chair across from me and said, "What happened? Why are you doing this? I don't want to separate—let's try to work this out."

I just stared at him, stunned. This is what always threw me. One minute he'd be ranting, the next pleading. I didn't know what to make of his erratic mood swings.

Somehow, no doubt by the grace of God, I got the courage to say what I was really feeling. "I think we just need some time apart. I can't live like this anymore."

And thus began round two, which went on for several hours. He'd blow up, then calm down. My body was shaking, and I couldn't control the swirling in my stomach. Once I ran to the bathroom and literally got sick to my stomach.

My marriage was burning to oblivion right in front of me, and I had no resources to step in and save it.

Twice that night Justin got in his car, peeled out of the apartment complex, and returned only to continue hurling hateful words at me.

The last time he slammed the door shut behind him, I heard the squeal of his tires as he drove off.

A couple of minutes later the phone rang and there he was on the line, screaming at me again. "I never want to see you again unless it's in a courtroom and I'm finished with you for good!"

That's when he did a "Whoa, whoa . . ." and I heard him hit the brakes. There was a thudding sound, then the phone went dead.

"Justin? Justin?" I shouted into the phone.

I was immediately on my knees, still crying. "God, please let him be okay. Please be with him. Please surround him with your protection," I pleaded. My stomach was one huge knot. "Please let him be okay," I whispered.

And then, as if on cue, I heard stomping up the apartment steps. There he was, storming through the door.

I was so flabbergasted I couldn't speak. How dare he fake the whole thing! He'd put on the drama full throttle, making me think he'd been in an accident just to scare me or get back at me.

I slumped on the couch as he started to shout again, berating me with his usual criticisms.

I sat there as he verbally waled on me, his arms thrashing as he paced back and forth. In the midst of his tirade, my mind tuned out his words as a terrifying thought overtook me: *What if we had children?*

I pictured a child in her bedroom, cowering under her covers to drown out the noise of her father letting loose. I pictured that little girl crying, scared and trembling. And I knew I could never put my son or daughter in that position.

I didn't want my children to hear their father threaten to leave someday. I might have been able to handle it, but my children would need stability and security. How could they cope if every time their dad got angry, they were plagued by the fear that their family would fall apart? I didn't want my son growing up thinking he had license to treat a woman—or anyone—with this kind of disrespect and abuse. And I didn't want my daughter growing up thinking this is what she should expect from a man.

Then came the moment of impact. The internal statement hit me with the force of a Mack truck: *If it wouldn't be right for them, Christi, then why are you still here?*

My mind paused for a second as I processed that statement.

Why are you *still here?*

And that was it. That was the moment I emotionally checked out. At that instant I was gone from the marriage—in my mind, at least.

When I came back from my cerebral fog, I heard Justin scream, "Do you really think there's someone better out there? Do you really want to be back out there, Christi?"

I thought, *No, I don't. But I certainly don't want to be here.*

Only part of my answer came out of my mouth. The "No, I don't" part.

He sat down and said, "Okay, then, let's think about this."

We went to bed, and I lay there wishing he'd just leave. Literally a couple minutes later, my wish came true. Out of the blue, he got up and said, "I can't be here. I can't do this!" And he walked out the door.

It was three in the morning, and I was alone. I sat in bed with the light on and picked up the phone. It was 6 a.m. in Ohio. I called Mom crying, and through my tears I told her what had happened. She asked if I was okay and if Justin was okay. Then she told me that she and Dad would support me no matter what happened.

After I hung up the phone, I crawled out of bed and lay down on the couch. I just couldn't be in that bed by myself—the bed that had been ours. Lying in it only amplified the fact that Justin's half of the bed was empty. It had been empty many times before, of course, but I knew this time was different.

I was too scared to turn off the lights and too rattled to sleep. As I lay there, the finality of it all started to sink in. I was alone.

In the still of the apartment, I could feel the end. It was like a locomotive that you hear off in the distance at first, but as it gets closer and closer, you can actually feel the ground trembling as it approaches.

Eventually I dozed off for about an hour or so. I awoke to the gradual light of the sunrise. When I went to the balcony, I could see the sun hovering on the edge of the downtown buildings and the palm trees, their feather-shaped leaves fanning in the breeze. I sat on the chair with my knees pulled to my chest. All I could do was pray. *What's going to happen?* I wondered. *What now?*

Oddly, an overwhelming sense of relief came over me. Yes, I was alone. But it was okay. In fact, it was better than okay. It was good. I suddenly found myself free of that ominous sense of "What will set him off today?"

I had peace.

Peace is hard to fake. We might be able to pull it off in front of someone else, but when it's just us and God, there isn't a lot of gray area. Either peace is there, or it's not.

And peace, I think, is connected to trust. Trust in God. Trust in yourself. Trust that whatever happens is manageable. Not fixable, mind you. But for the first time, I actually believed I might survive this mess.

I was amazed how immediately my body adjusted to the change. When I was with Justin in those moments of volatility, I couldn't repress the trembling and tenseness. But being there all by myself, my body felt peaceful again. My breathing was steady and deep, my muscles were relaxed, and I was enveloped in calm.

I called my friend Colleen and told her what happened, confessing, with a twinge of guilt, the peace I felt. The line beeped, indicating someone else was trying to call. Justin. I said good-bye to Colleen.

"Hello?"

"Hi," he said.

"Where are you?" I asked. "Are you okay?"

"Don't act like you care where I am. I stayed at a hotel last night."

Before I could even speak, he barreled on. "I've decided I'm filing for divorce. Irreconcilable differences. I've already contacted an attorney and found an apartment. I also called my boss and gave him two weeks' notice because I can't work near you. I called my agent, and he's working on it. Oh, and I called my parents."

My jaw was on the ground. I'd asked for some time apart—a separation—but apparently he saw this as all or nothing. He wasn't wasting any time.

Before I could even get a syllable out, his tone softened. "I just want to come home," he said. The next thing I knew, he was walking up the stairs. He came in, looked at me, and started crying.

"I can't do this again, Christi. Let's just work it out."

"What do you mean?" I asked. "You obviously already started the process! What did your parents say?"

"I didn't call them," he confessed.

"What do you mean? What about your agent? Your boss? The apartment? You didn't do any of that?"

"No. I just need to sleep."

I stood there dumbfounded. He had done nothing. Nothing, except spin more lies in an attempt to scare me.

He walked into the bedroom and crawled into bed.

We were both exhausted, but I couldn't bring myself to lie

down next to him. I didn't even want to be in the same room. I told him I needed some space and was going for a drive.

————•————

I drove to the church I'd been attending for the last couple of years and sat in the parking lot with the windows rolled down, watching as the sunshine splashed over the steeple.

How did I get here, God? How did my life come to this point where I'm sitting alone in a church parking lot looking for answers?

I called Nanette. My dear, sweet friend Nanny.

"Are you okay?" she asked as I relived the previous night for her.

"You know we've always believed things happen for a reason," she reminded me. "Whatever you're searching for, you can't ignore it now. It's too big." After a pause, she asked me how I was feeling.

"Like I've been pummeled. Every muscle in my body aches, and my head feels like it's going to explode. I'm so confused. It's like I'm fighting the truth—I know I have to leave, but I don't have a clue how to do it! Nan, I'm terrified!"

"Pray, Christi. You know that's how you'll get your answers. And I'm praying for you too! I love you."

I sat there awhile longer just staring at the church. Maybe I was waiting for Jesus Himself to walk out of those tall wooden doors, saunter over to my car, and say, "Snap out of it! Here's what you need to do. . . ." I know it sounds crazy, but what if God did show up? I was in the right place, after all, right? This sacred space where people come to worship, where crosses serve as a reminder that sins have been paid for, where there's an altar for people to fall to their knees and ask for forgiveness for the mess they've created.

"Trust in the Lord with all your heart and lean not on your own understanding." The words of Proverbs 3:5 popped into my head out of nowhere.

"My own understanding? I don't have any right now, God!" I whined.

"Trust in the Lord with all your heart. . . ."

Okay, I was getting it. Maybe that was part of my problem. I'd been seeing God as this distant entity—Someone who could fix all my problems except the ones I'd got myself into. Wasn't God mad at me? I mean, even I was mad at me! I was disappointed in myself. I didn't deserve to be happy.

Whoa. That got my attention. Where had that come from?

How could I trust God to take care of me when I didn't deserve it?

Trust in the Lord with all your heart. . . .

Sitting in the car with the windows rolled down and the desert breeze wisping through my hair, I realized something: I didn't trust God.

I mean, I'd been praying for four years that He'd save my marriage. I'd been begging Him to intervene and bridge this vast canyon between Justin and me. I'd been pleading with Him for so long, but where had it gotten me? To an empty church parking lot, feeling like a vagrant with no place to call home.

Healing is born when we get real with ourselves. No matter how ugly we're afraid that realness is.

This is where the real healing started. Healing, as I was learning, is born when we get real with ourselves. No matter how ugly we're afraid that realness is.

The healing might be undetectable at first—so minuscule and

meager that we don't even know it's there. But whether we sense it or not, it comes to life that moment we give up and finally say, "Okay. I've messed up. I'm willing to see this differently. Please help me do that, God."

And when healing begins, it gives way for miracles to emerge.

On that day, I was on the verge of a miracle myself. But I would have to go through some pretty messy muck before that miracle would become a reality.

I thought about the epiphany I'd had the night before, when I realized that if this relationship wasn't safe for a child, then it wasn't safe for me. In a flash, I recognized myself as the child in this situation . . . and God as the Father.

And just like I'd known emphatically that I'd do anything to protect my children, I realized that was exactly what God was doing for me. If I felt that way about children I didn't even have yet, imagine how fiercely protective God must be of me—His daughter.

My picture of God suddenly changed. I'd been taught to look at Him as Lord, but what about as Father? I so often saw Him as a judge, a disciplinarian, an omnipotent force that could blow the world apart with one swipe of His hand if He wanted to. But what about as Father? A gentle, compassionate, loving Father who so desperately wants to help but is patiently waiting for an opening. If I didn't surrender this whole catastrophe to Him, He wasn't going to swoop in and save the day without a welcome from me. He could, of course. But based on my experiences, God wants to be *invited*.

What God wants from us most is a relationship. He wants our trust. He loves to hear our voices calling to Him. He doesn't stand there with His hands on His hips pointing a finger at us when we make mistakes—He is right there ready to save us from ourselves and the messes we're in.

Well, I'd been so busy asking Him to save my marriage that I didn't stop to ask Him if this was where He wanted me in the first place. Maybe that's what Garth Brooks was talking about in his song "Unanswered Prayers." Maybe God was working the chess pieces of my life around right in front of me, but because they weren't moving the way I wanted them to, I got mad and withheld my trust. If God wasn't going to do it "right," then I'd do it myself! Yeah, because that had worked so beautifully for me thus far. Ha!

"God, where are you?" I whispered.

I didn't hear a reply, but I didn't feel so alone anymore. Maybe that was the moment I started seeing God as my Father as well as my Savior. I knew my earthly father would never abandon me or steer me wrong. So shouldn't I have even more trust that God the Father would be able to drive this bus for me? Now I just needed to take my own hands off the wheel. . . .

Ironically enough, I felt the urge to drive, so I started the car and drove to Encanto Park. It was a glorious day by weather standards. I sat on a bench near a fountain, and flowers bloomed all around me. I felt a surge of gratefulness for the vibrant pink poking out of the leaves of the bougainvilleas, for the constant trickle from the fountain, for the fresh breeze on my face.

I called Dr. Anderson and made an appointment. He said he was sorry for what I was going through and agreed to see me the next day.

Then I called Mom, who was aching for both me and Justin. She posed a question that forced me to be brutally honest with myself. "If you and Justin had stayed in West Virginia, do you think you would have gotten married?"

She left me to ponder that question as we hung up. The answer didn't take long for me to come to, and it crushed my spirit.

I couldn't say yes.

In fact, I realized I had married Justin not because I knew it would last forever, but because I feared that it wouldn't. Perhaps by marrying him, I'd thought I could make it last. Well, wasn't *that* a healthy mind-set?

I started thinking about how I'd gotten that job offer from Cleveland at the same time and shook my head, chuckling a bit. I had to believe God must have been shaking His head back then too! There He was, giving me another option other than marrying Justin, and I'd turned it down, basically saying, "It's okay, God. Really! I know what I'm doing."

Sure, I had asked God what I should do back then, but I'd never really stopped to listen for a reply. I never shut up long enough to allow Him to answer. I just ran full force toward my own bad idea and gave my life and myself to this man who, although he loved me, wasn't any better prepared to get married than I was.

It occurred to me that maybe this time I needed to shut my mouth. It was time to open my heart to whatever God had in store for me. As trite as it might sound, I needed to let go and let God.

So I sat there in silence, soaking in the serenity of my surroundings. I wanted to make this more about listening than making my own noise—internal or external. After about five minutes of silence, I prayed with every ounce of breath I had. "God, please help me. What should I say? Where do I go from here? Be with Justin. Be with me. Give us answers." As I sat there in the quiet, I felt a strength come over me. I had no firm answers about what the next action should be. So I did the only thing I knew to do: nothing. I went home. I let him sleep. I did some work. And we let this turmoil lie beneath the surface for a little while, knowing the truth would eventually come to light. But until I knew what God wanted me to do next, I decided to wait. That felt like the safest plan.

If we knew what was coming, there wouldn't be a need for faith.

Sometimes I wish that waiting weren't so hard. Clearly, if we knew what we were waiting for—if we had some reassurance that something wonderful was around the bend—the waiting wouldn't be so daunting.

But let's face it: that goes against the essence of what faith is. If we could see what was coming, then the waiting wouldn't be disciplining us, nudging us to trust God. We wouldn't experience the thrill of discovering that even if we're not doing anything, God is already in the game, strategically placing all the pieces where they'll be most effective.

When we fail to wait on God's timing, we can't confirm whether we're making the right decision. We just leap out of the plane with imaginary wings and no parachute.

My past is proof of that. I wanted to marry Justin, so I did despite my trepidations. Rather than sit on it for a while and give the idea some time to settle in, I gave myself four lousy days of back and forth. Cleveland or Justin? The job or the man? If I'm truly honest, I don't think I ever opened myself enough to hear someone else's thoughts about it, let alone God's. I knew what I was going to do the whole time—I was going to marry Justin. Those four days were really just my mourning the loss of a job I hadn't even rejected yet.

My mom told me years ago that if we knew what was coming, there wouldn't be a need for faith. And it's impossible to please God without it. Maybe waiting is God's way of bringing us closer to Him. This was His way of saying, "Lean on Me."

I heard once that the task of waiting is also God's way of purifying our motives. It forces us to ask ourselves, *Why am I making this decision?* Out of fear? Out of desperation? Out of greed or insecurity? None of those reasons are going to lead us to peace. We need to filter through our superficial motivations—pride, anger, betrayal—and examine why we want something. I needed to take some time to figure out why I wanted to leave this marriage. And that answer would only come through patience.

———•———

My next meeting with Dr. Anderson gave me the perspective I desperately needed.

I confessed the enormous guilt I felt when I thought about leaving Justin. I could already sense that the pain yet to come would take on a life of its own. The last thing I wanted to do was hurt him. I really believed he was a good man who was haunted by some demon he couldn't escape. Dr. Anderson helped me realize that, while Justin had his strong points, he also needed to take responsibility for what was happening to us, just as I did.

Each of us—Justin included—has the power to choose differently. Yes, he had alcohol issues. Yes, he was hiding behind some kind of pain. But he also had the capacity to face what was dragging him down. To change it. To choose differently. And so did I.

My dream of getting through to Justin and fixing our marriage started dripping away like the wax of a candle. We'd been through the fire in our marriage, but it hadn't made us stronger—it had melted us into a clump of hard wax that could no longer be molded into anything useful. At least not us together.

I became acutely aware that I couldn't choose differently on Justin's behalf. I couldn't make him less angry. I couldn't make him stop drinking. I couldn't make him stop lying. But I *could* choose whether I would enable him. I had to own the fact that my past avoidance of the situation was doing just that. And in doing so, I was hurting both of us.

Dr. Anderson helped me see this wasn't about blame, though. This lesson was about control—what was under my command and what wasn't. Could I force Justin to own up to his lies and booze-filled habits? No. Could I choose my reaction to those lies? Yes.

Although my counseling session did open my eyes to the fact that this was not where I wanted to be, I didn't yet have the confidence to do anything about it. I was consumed by the fear of what Justin might do to me or to himself if I left. How could I possibly escape this relationship without burning one of us?

The truth was, I couldn't. It was impossible to leave without both of us feeling the anguish of it. There would be so many suppressed feelings that would detonate, and I couldn't ignore that reality. But it wasn't as if they were going to dissipate if I stayed.

I told Dr. Anderson that on one hand I felt incredible guilt and shame for the hurt I would cause Justin. But I also felt angry about what had happened the other night, and I was afraid of Justin's temper. And the truth was, I didn't trust him. I didn't trust him not to hurt me. I didn't trust him not to drink. And I didn't trust him to be faithful. He was like Jekyll and Hyde. One minute he would be loving and wonderful, but a minute later his rage could strike for no apparent reason.

The bottom line, as I realized in Dr. Anderson's office, was that Justin could be so cruel it terrified me. And this much I now knew: I couldn't live like this.

I knew for certain it was time to leave. But I wasn't convinced I had the strength to do it at all.

—•—

That seesawing over my decision plagued me for the next few weeks. I walked through life like a zombie again, only this time it was worse because I was aware it was happening. I could feel myself slipping away, little by little. I was morphing into a body without a spirit. When I thought about leaving, I felt utterly paralyzed.

Have you ever had that dream where your legs are moving and you're trying to run, but you aren't going anywhere? No matter how hard you try, you can't get away from whatever it is you're trying to escape. That's how I felt.

You can only go on like that for so long before you crack.

After a few weeks the weight of it all buckled my knees again, and I found myself alone on the floor of our apartment, praying for forgiveness.

Forgiveness for everything. For hurting Justin. For not listening to God. For stealing that quarter from my dad's nightstand when I was eight years old so I could buy *Charlie's Angels* cards at the park's concession stand. I felt the need to repent for every sin I'd ever committed, even for the times I'd sinned and didn't know it.

There's a famous quote by Albert Einstein that defines insanity as doing the same thing over and over again and expecting different results.

Well, insanity was sitting on my front porch, pounding on the door to get in. I'd been doing the same things to fix my marriage for the past four years, and they simply weren't working. I was exhausted.

And so I prayed. I knew this was a critical moment. I could feel myself edging toward a nervous breakdown. Either I was going to continue traveling through life in denial, with all my feelings and emotions shut down, or I was going to risk life as I knew it and leave for a fresh start . . . alone.

Either scenario involved risk. The question was, which risk was greater? Which offered more potential for me to live authentically, even if that came in the long term, not immediately?

My voice sounded meek and fatigued as I prayed. "God, please show me what to do. If you want me to stay, give me the desire and the strength to do that and the ability to help Justin. If you want me to go, give me the wisdom to know that's the right thing to do and the courage to do it."

And then there were no words. That's all I had.

I couldn't even think of what else to ask for. I felt hollowed out somehow. When your plea is so desperate yet so deliberate, there's nothing left to hide behind. It's simply you on your knees, with a few tears rolling down your face. Searching for God. Searching for strength.

I don't know how much time went by, but I heard nothing—no

voice, no guidance, no stirring. Just calm. So I got up and started doing the dishes and the laundry. Back to the daily grind. As I walked into the guest bathroom to hang the freshly washed towels, it hit me. No, it pummeled me.

I stood there for a second trying to absorb what I was feeling. Suddenly there was peace. There was joy. And was it true? Yes! There was hope. I hadn't felt that for so long it was like running into an old friend. I'd been starving for it, and now here it was, standing firmly in my presence!

I didn't necessarily hear anything in my head like Gram did, but I do know that suddenly, out of nowhere, I had my answer. I knew what I needed to do. And although I feared the task ahead of me, I felt a comfort beyond understanding. There were no symphonies playing or trumpets blaring as I embraced this epiphany—it was just me in the bathroom, towels in hand, experiencing a cleansing of all that had been and a hope for all that was to come. The fear was still there, but for the first time the certainty of what I needed to do overpowered it.

Once you ask God for help, make no mistake—He gives it. He is right there with you the entire time, holding your hand and giving you the guidance you need. You may not feel it in that moment, but I can assure you He's there.

Once you ask God for help, make no mistake—He gives it. He is right there with you the entire time, holding your hand and giving you the guidance you need. You may not feel it in that moment, but I can assure you He's there.

Whatever needs to be done, God has equipped you to handle it. This is a new day. This is a new chance. This is a new choice you get to make—and God's got your back through it all.

CHAPTER 9

NEVER UNDERESTIMATE THE POWER OF FORGIVENESS

I WAS GETTING STRONGER. A conversation I had with Justin a few days later served as confirmation of that.

We started talking about where our relationship was going, and he laid into his favorite technique with me—deflection. He tried to transfer the blame from himself to me. "Christi, you were engaged in college, and you called that off too!" he shouted. "Maybe this is just a pattern for you. Maybe this is how you handle things!"

Now, had Justin said something like that months ago, I might have started doubting myself, questioning if there was credence to his accusation. But not now. Now I had the truth firmly planted on my side.

Yes, I'd been engaged in college—to a wonderful man named Scott, someone I still admire. After several months of wedding talk and discussing where we'd live and what we'd do career-wise, it was evident Scott and I had different goals. At the time I wanted to see the world. I'd interned at *Entertainment Tonight* in Hollywood, and I wanted to go back. As an engineering major, Scott had a great opportunity to stay in Ohio and settle into a promising career himself. I loved the city; he loved the country. We both wanted a family, but at twenty-one, I wasn't ready for that yet. Although he said he'd go to California with me, he didn't want to be there forever. But what if we went and I didn't want to leave?

I began to see that if I conformed to what he wanted to do, I'd be okay for a while, but I was afraid I'd eventually end up resenting him. And it wouldn't have been his fault. If he conformed to what I wanted to do, I was afraid he'd be miserable. The breakup wasn't easy on either of us, but in the end we both knew it just had to be.

One broken engagement didn't constitute "a pattern," as Justin alleged, and I knew it.

I was hardly the perfect wife, that's true. But I was confident enough to know I didn't have to take this. I wasn't in denial anymore. And if things were ever going to get better, Justin needed to take responsibility too. But I couldn't make him do that. It would have to be his choice.

Justin must have known on some level how serious things were, because he finally agreed to go back to Dr. Anderson with me. When we were at our first session together, I broached the subject of going home to see my parents for a week—by myself. I was desperate to get out of this environment. I needed somewhere I could think clearly and decipher how to move forward.

Justin was vehemently opposed to the idea. He argued that my parents didn't like him and would encourage me to leave him. I was dumbfounded by this. I knew he didn't like my father, but I couldn't believe he'd assume my family would coerce me into leaving him. If he only knew how often my parents had encouraged me to fight, to get help for our marriage.

Dr. Anderson said, "There's nothing wrong with Christi wanting to go home to see her parents. It's normal to want to be with your family. And the more you refuse to let her go, the more she'll eventually wind up resenting you for it."

It was a huge moment for me to have Dr. Anderson defend my right to see my parents. To hear a professional say that my desire to see my family was normal affirmed that I wasn't a weak little girl. After so many occasions of being berated and judged for longing to go home, it was freeing to hear someone validate me like that.

Justin scowled but relented. I made plans immediately and booked a ticket for the following week. I was elated.

———•———

A few days later I was back in Dr. Anderson's office alone, trying to figure out the best way to leave Justin. Dr. Anderson and I both believed this was the right timing, but there was so much to consider. I wanted to make sure I did this with as much integrity, consideration, and gentleness as possible. But is there a "right" way to leave your husband? Are there blueprints to guide you through such a difficult process? Is there a guidebook that tells you what you should and shouldn't do, what you should and shouldn't say? Nope. Just Dr. Anderson. And I thank God for him.

My biggest concern was trying not to hurt Justin. But there

was no avoiding the fact that it would. Dr. Anderson and I played out the scenarios.

Number one: should I tell him by myself at home? I was crippled by the thought of dropping this bomb on him when we were alone. What would he do to me? To himself? Would he get violent again? And how far might he take things when he realized this was for real?

If you've ever wondered why someone doesn't "just leave," this is why. If you're married to someone who goes ballistic over small matters, as Justin did, then you can only imagine what it would be like to sit down with that person and tell him something he doesn't want to hear. Something that's actually a big deal with a big consequence. That's why women don't "just leave," as people often suggest. Studies have shown that one of the most dangerous times for a person being abused is when she leaves. It's simply not as easy as packing up your bags.

So choice number one seemed impossible.

Number two: should I call his parents and have them be there when I broke the news? The problem with that possibility was that I didn't want to humiliate Justin by having someone else there when I told him. I didn't want him to feel disrespected—to experience the shame of having everyone in the room know this was coming except him. I felt like I should at least give him the dignity of being the first to know I was leaving him.

Number three: should I call him from Ohio when I was home with my parents? I didn't want to take what might be perceived as the easy way out and avoid facing him in person. But at least I'd be thousands of miles away and out of physical danger if the confrontation escalated. And based on past experiences, chances were it would.

I sat on these options for a few days, vacillating between them all. What happened next convinced me that, yes, God had my back.

As I was still considering the next step, Justin's mom called and told me Justin's brother, Jeff, was coming to be with him while I was in Ohio. She said she knew things had "intensified" between us and that Justin needed help. Her hope was that Jeff's calm, logical demeanor could be that help in some way.

At that moment I wanted to forewarn her of my decision. I didn't want Jeff coming out here blind to what was about to happen. But that didn't feel fair to Justin. I decided it was only right for me to let him tell them once I dropped the bombshell myself.

Of course, there was no telling what Justin's version of things would be, but I couldn't worry about that. So in the end, I simply told my mother-in-law how grateful I was to know Jeff would be here. Oh, if only she knew.

The news of Jeff's visit felt like the nudge I was looking for. I would go home to Ohio and let Justin know of my decision by phone. That way I'd be physically safe from his wrath, and Jeff would be there to help Justin through it.

I made plans to stay with my friend Carey from work when I returned to Arizona if I needed a place to go. I wasn't sure if Justin would move or if he'd want me to get out, so I made arrangements just in case. I packed enough clothes for two weeks rather than just the one I'd be in Ohio.

I'm thankful to God for Carey. I knew I was putting her in an uncomfortable position since she was friends with Justin, too, but she graciously opened her home to me. I hadn't shared much with her about what was happening between Justin and me. She had a strong maternal instinct and good gut intuition, though, and it turned out that she had suspected for a long time that things weren't right at home. Her unwavering support was monumental to me.

On the afternoon I flew to Ohio, the sun was shining brightly, just as it had on our wedding day. But now I was leaving.

As Justin dropped me off at the airport, I said good-bye with the gut-wrenching sense that this was it. It was followed by a wave of guilt that *he* didn't know that.

Justin clearly wasn't happy about dropping me off. He didn't approve of this trip home, and he didn't make any attempt to hide it. I don't think we even kissed good-bye.

As I walked toward the glass doors of the airport, I took one look back at him as he got in the car. He never turned back. He didn't wave good-bye.

I stepped through the airport doors, my bag in tow, and let out a huge sigh—the kind that comes from deep in your gut—and I felt relief sweep through my entire body. It was as though I was finally inhaling fresh air again. I was free. I was on my own. And that was perfectly okay.

When you've been locked in a relationship that doesn't allow you to be who you really are, suddenly being alone isn't a bad thing. It's a blessing.

On the plane ride home I went over and over in my mind what I'd say to Justin when I called him in a couple of days. I'd have to choose my words intentionally and be careful of my tone. I wanted to do this as gently as possible—not because I was scared, but because I wanted Justin to be okay. As I looked out the window at the blue sky and puffy clouds floating beside us, I realized I felt no anger. No animosity. I did feel sadness, though—especially since I knew things would get much worse before they got better. But I saw Justin the way I used to see him. I loved him, though I wasn't *in love* with him. I wanted him to be happy.

"God, please help us through this. Help him be okay," I whispered.

———•———

I stepped off the plane in Cleveland and was overwhelmed when I saw my parents waiting for me. Elation and relief swooshed through my body as my mom put her arms around me. On the one hand, I felt like a kid safely enveloped in my mother's arms. On the other hand, I felt like a grown-up firmly standing on my own, with the future stretched in front of me. There was nothing to hinder my dreams, no barrier to stop me, no one to knock down my ideas with judgment or ridicule.

My parents, my brother, and sweet Gram took me to dinner that night. Before the meal came, Gram asked the big question: "How are things with Justin?" She said it nonchalantly, oblivious to what was happening.

I took a deep breath. "Gram . . . I'm leaving him," I said. "But I know this is the right thing." We all sat still, waiting for her reaction. I think it took her a second to process. Then right there, in the middle of the restaurant, she looked at me and started crying.

This completely threw me for a loop . . . and it broke my heart. Mom jumped in. "It's okay, Mom. This is what she needed to do. It really is for the best." Dad and I reassured her too. Danny just sat there—the poor guy didn't know what to say.

In the car on the way home Gram and I talked a lot, and by the end of the evening, we both had our own revelations.

For her part, she accepted that this was the best thing for me. She told me she wanted me to be safe and happy. And I understood that she was crying not just because I was leaving my husband but because she knew firsthand what I'd been going through the past four years. She absorbed how bad things must have been if I needed to leave my marriage, and she ached that I had to go through this.

When we got home, Mom and I sat on the couch talking before heading to bed. She told me she'd confided in her friend Sherl about what was going on and why I was coming home. Sherl had gone through a divorce after being married for a long time, and she was now happily married to a wonderful man who adored her. Her newfound happiness was an example to me of what could be— that while this was a difficult chapter, good times and a healthy relationship could still be within reach.

When you have a mountain to climb, waiting isn't going to shrink it.

"When I told Sherl about what you've been through and why you were coming home, her response was, 'If Christi decides to leave, please tell her not to wait twenty-five years like I did.'"

What an image! Sherl's advice rang in my ears for days. I couldn't fathom waiting another twenty-one years to make this decision. I didn't want to waste that time holding on to something that wasn't going to get any better.

I pondered her statement throughout the night: *Please don't wait twenty-five years like I did.* It made me realize that when you have a mountain to climb, waiting isn't going to shrink it. It's only going to waste precious time—time in your life you can't get back.

I tried to be open and imagine whether things could get better with Justin. But one thing kept coming back to me: he chose a lie over me. I had given Justin three chances to own up to that two-hundred-dollar bar bill. And let's be honest—we both knew it wasn't about the money at all. It was about three openings to admit he had a problem. Three opportunities to come clean so we could move forward. Three chances to say, "You're important enough to me that I'll do whatever it takes to keep you."

When it came down to it, he knew our marriage depended on his commitment to telling me the truth, and he still chose not to. That made a big statement about what he valued. His image meant more to him than the truth, and his alcohol meant more to him than I did. I didn't want to be someone's second choice anymore.

As upside down as it sounds, the next several days were filled with joy. I reveled in the safety and freedom that surrounded me when I was with my family. I went running, I listened to music, I wrote in my journal. I basked in the security of home. But in the back of my mind, I knew I still had a phone call to make.

———◆———

It was late at night, and my parents had gone to bed. I was sitting there just staring at the phone.

Dread permeated every inch of me. No one was forcing me to make the call. There was no hard mandate that I had to say the words. But I knew in the depths of my soul that this was necessary. I had to do this—and do it in this moment. I'd been held back by fear long enough, and I wasn't going to let it stop me now.

I shot up a quick prayer and dialed slowly and deliberately.

"Hello?" Justin said.

"Hey. It's me."

There was some small talk. "Are you having a good time with Jeff?" "What have you been doing?" Then he asked if I'd been thinking about things.

Yes. I had.

"Justin, I'm not coming back. I mean, I'm coming back to Phoenix, but I can't keep living like this. I can't come back to you right now. I can't pretend things are okay when they're not. I hope you can understand that."

He didn't fly off the handle immediately. In fact, the conversation was somewhat civil at first. Maybe he hadn't quite absorbed what I'd said. Then it started.

"I can't believe you're doing this!" he shouted. "There's no separation here, Christi! It's divorce!"

"Okay." I tried to keep my voice calm.

"And don't think you're just getting out of this! I'm entitled to half of your 401(k)! Especially since I cashed mine out thinking we were going to use it as a down payment on a house! And what about the cars?"

"We'll deal with it," I said. I knew now wasn't the time to start arguing over material possessions.

He repeated, "This is divorce, Christi!"

When he finally took a breath, I said, "I have another place to stay for a bit when I get back, or if you don't want to be there, I understand. Just let me know what you want to do. If you want me to stay in the apartment, I will."

He told me there was no way he was staying there and that he'd be gone by the time I came home.

"I'm sorry, Justin. I hope someday you can understand."

"Tell that to my lawyer," he hissed.

"I'll talk to you later to work out details." We said a quick good-bye . . . and it was done. I placed the receiver back in the cradle and sat there waiting for something to happen.

I waited to feel the lump in my throat and the sting of tears in my eyes. I was ready for my body to tremble or for remorse to sweep over me. But none of that came. Not during the conversation, and not now. The tears I expected never fell.

What I felt instead was relief.

It was over. I'd said the words, and I knew there was no going back. But that was okay because I didn't want to go back. I wanted to be right where I was. In this chair in the middle of the night, alone.

Still, I felt heartsick about what I was putting Justin through— and his brother, for that matter.

I wondered what Justin was doing right then—how he was reacting, what he was saying to Jeff. I could only guess how much Jeff hated me. Then it suddenly hit me that maybe now Jeff would see the Justin I'd seen—the erratic, belligerent man who's impossible to reason with. And maybe on some level at least, Jeff would understand. Not that I expected him to defend me, mind you. But I wished someone in his family would understand, even a little. On some small level they'd think, *Oh, okay, I get it. I can see why she left.*

Yet I knew in all probability that I was going to be the bad guy in all this. As I processed things, though, it occurred to me that even if his family placed the full blame on me, that was okay too. And that surprised me because I've never been good at being the bad guy. I was the one who wanted everyone to like me, who wanted everyone to get along.

I knew that my decision wouldn't just hurt Justin; it would hurt his family, too—these people I had come to love over the past several years. The lines had officially been drawn—even though I'd give anything for an eraser. But for the first time in my life, I was okay with being the "guilty one." I'd certainly rather live with that than keep living the way I had the last few years.

The next morning Mom asked how it went with Justin and how I felt. Then she looked at me and said, "Christi, you need to be with someone who cherishes you."

I knew full well what she meant. Mom wasn't saying I should be pampered or spoiled or get everything I wanted. She was saying that I should be with a man who loved me and treated me that way. Someone who was considerate of me. Someone who treated me with respect. Someone who cherished me. I couldn't even dream about that at the moment.

That night I went running and stopped by Gram's place.

"How're you doing, hon?" She squeezed my hand.

"I'm really good, Gram. I feel free."

"I have to tell you, Christi, I knew at your wedding reception that this wasn't right."

I just sat there with my mouth open for a minute. Finally I could get out, "How?"

She paused, stared into the sky, then looked right at me. "I never saw him give you any affection that day," she said. "In fact, I've never seen him show affection toward you the whole time you've been married."

I could see that although she hated what I was going through, she understood this on a personal level. And she had her own fears about it all.

"Christi, don't go to that apartment by yourself when you get back. I don't want you to get hurt."

Once again, I was struck by her insight. Gram never knew about any of the verbal abuse or threats from Justin. She only knew he'd been "mean" and that he drank, but I'd never told her anything more. I didn't want to worry her. But it was clear she knew a lot more about what was happening than I'd given her credit for.

"I won't, Gram," I reassured her.

———•———

Back in my room at my parents' house, I sat on my bed and explored what was in my heart. I had expected to feel anger and resentment toward Justin. But to my surprise, I discovered I wasn't mad at him. Not anymore.

Now, I also knew there was a lot ahead of us, and I wasn't foolish enough to think everything would be smooth and agreeable from that point on. But at the core of me, I truly wanted him to be okay. I didn't want him to hurt anymore, and I didn't want him to be angry. I wanted him to find the truth for himself and be free from whatever was making him so hostile. I wanted him to feel what I was feeling: freedom.

That's what forgiveness does. It evokes freedom.

It's impossible to underestimate the power of forgiveness. My mom taught me that lesson years ago. It was a learning experience I'll treasure my whole life—but it was also a painful one.

I was in high school, and there was a girl I'll call Felicia (only because I know no one from high school by that name, so I can't get myself in trouble). To put it bluntly, Felicia hated my guts. I don't think it's an exaggeration to say that if I'd been standing in the middle of the parking lot and she had access to a truck, she would have mowed me down.

I couldn't exactly avoid her, though, since we were on the same cheerleading squad. Things came to a head one evening at a football game, shortly after our official cheerleading photo was taken. She was mad at me because she'd been absent for the picture, and the football program hadn't included a line in the program about her being missing from the photo. Because I was there when it was taken, apparently it was all my fault. You know—the usual teenage drama.

That night at the game, I finally confronted her. I felt I had to if we were going to spend the rest of the season together.

"Felicia, I'm sorry," I said. "I don't get what happened between us, but what do you say we just forget it all and start over as friends?"

What happened next stuck with me for a long time.

She looked me up and down, shook her head, chuckled, and walked away. In front of everyone! I was humiliated. I could feel my face burning with embarrassment as I heard the whispering around me. Several people said, "I can't believe she just did that to you!"

I went home fuming. I told my mom what had happened—how

degraded I felt and how angry I was. And I knew I had a right to be mad! Mom listened to my diatribe without interrupting. Then, very calmly, she said, "Christi, do you know what you have to do?"

I quieted down, waiting for the words of wisdom my mother was going to bestow on me—some brilliant piece of advice that would make everything right again. I knew she'd back me up on this.

"You have to forgive her."

Huh? *I'm sorry—can you repeat that? I must have misunderstood you. Surely I didn't hear what I thought I heard.*

She said it again. "You have to forgive her."

I stomped up to my room and vented with all the teenageness I could muster. I paced. I cried. Seriously, how could I forgive someone who had publicly humiliated me? And wasn't my mom supposed to be on my side?

As the days wore on, though, I realized Mom was right. Oh, don't you just *hate* that?

But what I hated more was how my anger was affecting me. It made me anxious and a bit paranoid. Whenever I was in the same room with Felicia

I realized that when you forgive someone, you unchain yourself from the anger that's clinging to you. Suddenly your world is wide open.

and she giggled, I was convinced she was making fun of me. I was realizing just how toxic anger is, and I didn't want that poison anymore.

A couple of years later, there was an incident where Felicia treated me horribly at a party one Friday. The following Monday I saw people coming to my defense, and I think it woke her up.

She asked *me* to forgive *her*. Now that was something I never saw coming, but I didn't think twice. I could tell she was being genuine and was truly sorry for how she'd hurt me. While I didn't let my guard down altogether, I did forgive her. I chose to give her the benefit of the doubt . . . and it felt fabulous!

I realized then that when you forgive someone, you unchain yourself from the anger that's clinging to you. Suddenly your world is wide open.

An unexpected twist to the story came several years later, when we were both in college and home on Christmas break. Felicia and I went to dinner together, and it turned out she'd become a Christian. She told me, "Christi, I don't know how you put up with me in high school. I was really horrible to you. But the way you forgave me was such an example to me. It really affected me."

When you forgive someone, it doesn't mean you're condoning what that person did to you. It doesn't mean you dismiss the person's behavior or ignore the consequences you're left to deal with. It means you're finished holding on to your own anger and resentment.

In that moment I learned another important lesson about forgiveness: even if we don't see the results immediately, we can never underestimate its power—both in our own lives and in the lives of the people we forgive.

But I wasn't in high school anymore, and this wasn't just a classmate. This was my husband. The battle felt much more brutal. More consequential.

And let's face it: it was.

I wasn't in a safe place with Justin, and I didn't believe I ever could be. A big part of me was angry about that. I'd trusted him more times than I could count, and almost every time I gave him an inch, he took a mile and then tried to cover his tracks. I felt used and bitter and beaten. And I didn't want that anymore.

There was one thing that made my choice to forgive him easier, however: I understood that when you forgive someone, it doesn't mean you're condoning what that person did to you. You're not saying, "It's okay that you hurt me." It doesn't mean you dismiss the person's behavior or ignore the consequences you're left to deal with. And it doesn't mean you absolve the person of his or her own responsibility to get it together. That's their journey, not yours.

It means you're finished holding on to your own anger and resentment, because at that point you're just punishing yourself. We have to learn to value ourselves enough to say to the one who hurt us, "What you think of me doesn't define me. What you do to me won't destroy me. I'm choosing to let this go so I can be free of all that toxicity." If we don't do that, we give our transgressor far too much power over our lives—even if that person is no longer around.

You can't get past a hurt until you're willing to say, "I forgive you because I know you're human, just like me." We need to recognize the humanness in others while still recognizing what's good for us and what's not. Our healing is directly intertwined with our capacity to forgive. It's a choice.

I knew I had to forgive Justin completely, because if I didn't release the anger, I would just be torturing myself. I'd already given four years of my life to this tumult. I wasn't giving it one more day, if I could help it.

We had both been hurt in this relationship. We were both furious, though for different reasons. But anger is anger. It's venomous. Healing would only come when we acknowledged that we were both guilty but also both capable of receiving forgiveness.

The other caveat about forgiveness was that it didn't mean I had to let Justin back in. This realization was huge for me because I'd always imagined that forgiveness resulted in a big hug fest. "Oh, I'm sorry!" "I'm sorry too!" Hug, hug, kiss, kiss. No—forgiving doesn't equate to naive vulnerability. It doesn't mean you have to invite the person who hurt you back to a place where he could hurt you again. It doesn't mean you have to keep him in your circle of friends. You can forgive someone and still cut that person out of your life. Just because you forgive the one who hurt you, it doesn't make that person suddenly safe for you.

You can forgive someone and still cut that person out of your life. Just because you forgive the one who hurt you, it doesn't make that person suddenly safe for you.

That realization was a watershed moment for me. It meant I no longer had to sit there and take it when Justin lashed out at me. I could say, "I forgive you. I wish you the best. Now go on your way—we don't have anything left to discuss here."

Some people view forgiving others as a weakness. They think it makes you vulnerable, even ignorant. But it's really one of the bravest choices you can ever make.

I also had to recognize how my own pride was an obstacle too. I could forgive Justin all I wanted, but that didn't guarantee he'd accept it. It didn't mean he'd even acknowledge my forgiveness.

I had to choose to forgive him anyway.

He might never feel remorse for what happened. He might never take responsibility for his part in it. He might never appreciate my efforts or accept my forgiveness. And my happiness couldn't be connected to whether he did. I wasn't responsible for how he responded. I was only responsible for what I could control—my own choices.

Sometimes we think we won't be able to fully heal until we hear someone own his or her part in what happened, until we hear the words "I'm sorry."

But waiting for such a moment we can't control is just setting ourselves up for another disappointment. It's giving that person far more power over us than he or she deserves.

Forgiving Justin didn't mean I had to stick around to see whether he'd find forgiveness himself. Again, that was his journey. Not mine.

We're not responsible for how someone responds to our forgiveness. We're only responsible for what we can control—ourselves.

Once I recognized this, I noticed how my bitterness slipped away.

I wasn't resentful.

I just needed to get out.

CHAPTER 10

PAIN IS TEMPORARY; HOW TEMPORARY IS UP TO YOU

THE NEXT DAY I drove to visit one of my friends who lived about half an hour away from my parents. On the ride home, I was feeling lighter than ever. My windows were down, and I was simply enjoying the brisk autumn air as it blew my hair all over the place.

My peace was interrupted by the ringing of my cell phone.

"I've thought about it, and I'm not leaving this apartment," Justin said. "If you want out, you can find a new place."

"Okay. If that's what you want, that's what I'll do. I will need to stop and get the car, though."

We agreed that he'd be gone when that happened. He was pretty reasonable during that conversation, and I was immediately grateful for Jeff. I sensed it was his stability that was helping Justin. It was odd, however, to hang up the phone and not say, "I love you," as we almost always had—up until last night.

As I drove to my parents' house, I made a mental list of what I needed to do. I knew there were precautions I should take to protect myself financially. Justin's calmness during our conversation, though refreshing, was also peculiar. It made me wonder if he was up to something.

When I got to my parents' house, I sat down and checked items off the monetary laundry list. First, I called our credit card company and asked them to take me off the account. I let them know I was responsible for the current charges on our joint card, but after this date, I'd no longer be bound to future purchases. Check one.

Next, I called our bank and opened my own checking account. Check two.

Then I called our real estate agent, the one we'd worked with in the past to look for a house. This was going to be interesting.

"I'm looking for a rental," I told her.

That threw her for a loop. "What do you mean? I thought you and Justin were looking to purchase a home."

"Well, the rental is just for me."

After I briefly explained my new situation, she was quiet for a second, then said, "I can't say I'm surprised, Christi. I could tell that something just didn't feel right. Don't take this the wrong way, because I think the world of you both, but I just never really understood your pairing."

Yet again, someone else was on to us before I even admitted it to myself! I told her what kind of place I was looking for and the area I preferred. We hung up with an appointment for the next week to check some things out. Check three.

Then came the call that stirred up mixed feelings in me. On the one hand, it made me shudder to think about having this conversation. But on the other hand, I wanted to hear her voice. I forced myself to exhale as the phone rang.

"Hello?" It was Justin's mother, Anna.

"Hi, Mom."

"Hi, Christi."

"Have you talked to Justin?"

"Yes. He told us everything."

"I'm so sorry," I said.

And that's when it happened. My eyes started stinging, my throat closed up, and the tears began streaming down my face.

"I know I'm the bad guy," I said. "But I can't deal with the anger and the outbursts. I just can't do it anymore."

"Well, it's going to take us a while to understand all of this," she said.

I told her I loved them all very much.

"We love you, too. That's why this is so hard."

"I'm so sorry." My voice was trembling.

"I'm sorry too."

There was an awkward silence as neither of us knew what to say next.

We agreed we'd talk later and said good-bye.

I hung up, took a deep breath, and there it came, the sobs racking my body. I had hurt her. I had hurt Justin's whole family.

Through the turbulence of the last four years, Anna had given me strength. She had stood up for me. I knew she wasn't blind to what had been happening. But now . . . I could hear the strain in her voice, and it hurt me to know I'd caused her pain. It hit me that I wasn't just saying good-bye to Justin; I was losing his family, too.

I recalled something Dr. Anderson had said to me during one of our sessions. "The breakup of a relationship is like an amputation," he said. "A part of your life has been cut off. A part of you is gone, and sooner or later you'll feel it. And often it'll be when you least expect it. It's something that might just hit you out of nowhere."

I hadn't felt that loss, that amputation, until now.

As the day wore on, I recognized that this was where my faith intersected with my support system: they both helped hold me up. My aunts and a few friends called, giving me their reassurance that they were behind me and that they loved me. My mother had alerted her prayer warriors that I was in need. Then there were the people who "just happened" to call at the very moment I needed a kind word or a little boost. I'm convinced those weren't coincidences—they were glimpses of God in action.

And when I called Carey to let her know I needed that extra room in her apartment, she said, "It's ready and waiting for you!"

It had never dawned on me as I was feeling so alone, making this torturous decision to leave Justin, that I would find this kind of support on the other side. When you're facing an end point like that, failure is what dominates your vision. If bliss is the cover photo on a wedding album, then defeat is the featured photo on the album of divorce.

But I was beginning to see things through a different lens. That snapshot of failure was transforming into an image of hope, and I was seeing the truth—that hope does not disappoint.

If I was going to truly embrace that hope, I had to be honest with myself about what was happening.

One, I was not going to play the victim here.

Okay. So I'd suffered. Who hasn't? Who hasn't been hurt or betrayed or even devastated at some point in his or her life? I was brought to my knees by my pain, yes, but it hadn't killed me. And I knew the abuse I experienced was minute compared to what some people go through.

I refused to fall into the trap of feeling sorry for myself because if I did that—if I played the victim—I was only letting self-doubt have the last word.

I knew I had to take responsibility, to own my part. I cut Justin off emotionally. I allowed myself to shut down. I stopped seeing my marriage as forever. I was resentful at times. I'm sure my sadness was palpable—even to Justin. I was far from a perfect wife, but I knew if I stayed I might well become a Stepford one. A plastic, apathetic shell walking around like a mechanized doll. That was no way to live.

Pain is temporary. How *temporary is up to us.*

As I'd learned the hard way, pain is not the worst thing that can happen to us. I'd rather feel pain than feel nothing at all. Faith tells us that at some point the pain will subside and make way for something better. Something beautiful. The more we keep the faith, the more we'll recognize that God is working for us—and we'll understand what He wants us to do. We can take to heart that famous promise about hope:

> Now faith is being sure of what we hope for and certain
> of what we do not see.
>
> HEBREWS 11:1

If we concentrate on the pain, it's awfully hard to see the hope. Pain is temporary. *How* temporary is up to us.

We can't immerse ourselves in our pain and simultaneously stand in power. It just isn't possible to do both. Yes, we can feel the pain. We can remember the anguish. It's not going away overnight. But wallowing in it doesn't bring us back to dignity or integrity.

I refused to be a victim. I was a woman who had made a choice that brought me to a place that hurt. We all do that. What's important is that when we do, we work to correct it.

Two, I realized I wasn't alone. I had been so caught up in what this would do to me, to Justin, and to our families that I didn't recognize the reinforcements that had been there for me along the way. My best friends, Nanette and Jen. My parents. My grandmas. We're never left helpless—even if that's how we feel.

Of course, no one can predict how others will react to the news that you're leaving your husband. Thinking about the conversations people will have is enough to make even the most confident person feel self-conscious and insecure. But you're not the first person to ever walk this battle line. All of us have struggles we're trying to conquer. We need to remember that at the end of the day, God is always there for us, and He always provides someone else who cares about us too. That's one of His greatest gifts in moments like these—the reminder that we're not alone. It's hard to see it when the isolation and loneliness feel so encompassing. But that's all the more reason to keep our eyes open for those reminders.

We all have pasts. We all have stories. We all have skeletons. And we all have opportunities to make a fresh start. The thing about tragedy is that it reveals who is faithfully there for us and who isn't. And as much as it might hurt to realize someone we thought we could count on might not have our best interests at heart, it is cleansing. It releases us from the people who aren't strong enough to stand up for us, who aren't loyal enough to stick with us, who aren't confident enough to celebrate with us.

The superficiality drains away, and that torturous road we're walking makes us even more grateful for the people who do stay by our side, even through the uncertainty of where we're going.

———•———

On the wall of my old room at home, a few pictures from high school still hung on a corkboard. Brenda and me at a football game. Jen and me at her house. I thought of something another friend often told me: "I'm so impressed with the effort and time you put into your friendships, Christi."

It struck me as funny because I don't see it that way. I've just learned to love the people I can count on. The people I can be real with—and who know they can be real with me. It's really not that complicated. When you've been betrayed or deeply hurt by someone, you learn how to spot those people who aren't worthy of your trust. But you also become aware of the people you should be grateful for.

There I was, severing a sacred connection with my husband, and despite the brokenness, I was also feeling incredibly blessed. Blessed because I was not alone. It was in that challenging season that I realized how enveloped I was by my loyal, trustworthy, forever army of companions.

One thing they couldn't do for me, though, was the work I needed to do on myself. The big questions I needed to answer now were, Why did I stay? Why did it take me so long to see the truth? I knew these answers would take some introspection, and that was going to mean work. But it was critical if I was going to find healing and avoid this route in the future.

As I looked around my bedroom, where so many stories of my teenage years were archived, a whole new tale was taking shape now, fourteen years later. From sixteen-year-old heartbreaks to the heartache of divorce—no matter how old we get, our hearts are still vulnerable and our life lessons are still calling for us to get real and pay attention.

I knew one of the reasons I hadn't left before was because marriage was sacred to me. But here's what knocked me on my heinie when I looked the situation square in the eye: I was never really willing to go. Sure, I'd prayed and asked God what to do. But until I was truly open to His guidance, I hadn't been able to hear an authentic answer. Just like a teenager who asks for advice then bolts out the door and does her own thing anyway, I'd posed the question to God—but only rhetorically. Until I was open to hearing whatever He said—even if it was excruciating—I wasn't going to make any real progress. *Real* being the key word here.

When we don't face the pain, we aren't escaping it. We're only prolonging it.

Now I yearned for that genuine experience of just being me. I wanted people around me who were real, with no pretension. No charades. No masks or false pretexts. I wanted to live the truth, even if that truth was painful, because at least it was real.

I'd lived for four years trying to make the lies of my marriage true. But it's impossible to transform fallacies into reality; we only wind up distorting the truth in an attempt to make it less painful. It might work—for a minute. But the longer we run from the truth, the more miserable we're going to be. When we don't face the pain, we aren't escaping it. We're only prolonging it.

I was done running. I had no idea what my truth was going to look like from this point on, but I was finally ready to embrace it. Part of that road toward truth was learning to see myself differently.

It would take time. It would take work. It would take faith. But I was willing to give it a try. I was willing to hear whatever guidance God had for me. And this time I was ready to follow through with it.

CHAPTER 11

IN THE SILENCE, FIND YOUR STRENGTH

IT WAS NINE o'clock in the evening by the time my plane landed in Phoenix. The moment I inhaled the desert air, my anxiety started to intensify. I grabbed a taxi and fretted the whole way to our apartment. Would Justin hold up his end of the deal and be gone when I arrived to get my car keys? I walked up the steps and saw that one of the lights in the apartment was on. My heart started beating wildly. What was I walking into?

As I turned the key, I braced myself. But as I pushed the door open, I saw the living room was empty. Something seemed different, although I couldn't put my finger on what it was.

He'd obviously done some cleaning. It smelled nice, like a candle had been lit. And there was a note for me on the kitchen counter:

Christi,

*Here are the keys. Dr. Anderson told me it would be good
for me not to be home, so I'll talk to you later.*

Justin

I was stunned. He'd talked to Dr. Anderson! Was he actually making an effort? His words contained no nastiness, no insult, no anger. I turned the paper over. Was I missing something? But no, the back was blank.

I looked around the apartment at how beautiful and comfortable it seemed. I loved the way the city lights glistened outside the windows at night. It felt peaceful—at this instant, anyway. I stood there for a moment, taking it in. A moment was all it took before I snapped out of it. I wanted to get out of there before Justin returned, and I didn't know how much time I had.

After throwing a few more things in my bag, I grabbed the car keys and walked down the stairs. It was then that I looked more closely at the keys in my hand. I couldn't believe it! He'd left me the keys to *his* car—the one that was not nearly as nice as mine. Oh yeah, he'd taken my car. Go figure. I knew that note was too good to be true! This was his way of getting in another jab at me. I felt like he was saying, "Do what you want, Christi, but I've still got control here!" I fumed for about fifteen seconds, but then I smiled. Who cares! He can have the car. I've got my freedom.

I drove to Carey's and let myself in since she was on a date. I went to my room and noticed she'd made up the guest bed and left a sweet note for me. She had laid out books and magazines on the nightstand, and there were fresh flowers on the desk. Bath towels were neatly folded on the counter in the bathroom. This was truly the Carey Resort!

I turned on the TV to watch the news. I had to know what I'd missed since I'd been gone . . . but I couldn't concentrate. I couldn't help feeling totally displaced.

As beautiful and welcoming as Carey's home was, it wasn't my home. In fact, I felt homeless. Like a vagrant. I was suddenly enveloped by this unsettled, awkward sensation. Where was I? Obviously, I knew where I was physically, and I was incredibly grateful for a place to stay. But I no longer had anywhere to belong. No home base. No place to call my own. I hadn't been prepared for how much that would rattle me.

I was feeling the amputation like never before. It made sense, I suppose—everything I'd known to be my life for the past four years was disintegrating. And perhaps even more than the loss of home, I was realizing that I'd spent the last four years feeling like I had no emotional home base. Sure, I'd always had a place to hang my hat but no place to rest my heart.

Seriously, Christi! What do you want? I began to berate myself until I realized it wasn't my voice I heard badgering me. It was Justin's.

At that moment I knew the luggage at the end of the bed wasn't the only baggage I was carrying around. I may have physically taken myself out of the situation, but emotionally I still had a long way to go.

———•———

It was time to get back to work, but it wasn't the distraction I hoped it would be. Justin was calling me at night, giving me grief about our separation. He vilified me for leaving, accusing me of being selfish and apathetic. He kept badgering me about money—what was his, what was mine, what we needed to sort out. It was exhausting.

I sat down with Dr. Anderson that week and told him I was ready to file for divorce. He urged me not to go there yet.

"Let's give you a little time to settle into where you are before you make any permanent decisions."

"But I do feel like I'm ready," I told him. "I don't want to drag this out. I know I can't go back to him. Not the way things are."

I took a breath. "I really want to do this with integrity and honesty. I want to be as gentle as possible with Justin, but I don't want to lie to him either. I just don't see this going any further. What do you think I should do?"

Dr. Anderson reminded me how raw my emotions were at this point, and he recommended that I not make any quick decisions I'd regret later. He also told me Justin wanted to work things out, although he was still being irrational.

"He's dealing with a lot too," Dr. Anderson said. "I think you should tell him at this point you want to continue the separation. Let him get used to that idea before we broach the idea of divorce. Let's give him some time and see if he can step up and change."

"The funny thing is, I heard our wedding song on the radio the other day," I said. "It only made me cringe. Aren't I supposed to be feeling some sort of regret over this separation? I'm sad, of course, but that's just because Justin is hurting. Not because we're apart."

Dr. Anderson looked right at me. "You know, Christi, at some point you'll feel it. It might not be a special song you shared or an image of him. I don't know what it will be. But eventually something will prompt a twinge of regret, and you won't be able to deny it. That doesn't mean you're making a mistake by separating. It just means you're human and you still care about Justin's well-being."

I wondered what would prompt that hesitation, if it came at all.

A couple of nights later, I found myself sitting in Dr. Anderson's office with Justin across from me.

"Okay," Dr. Anderson started, "how are you feeling about things, Christi?"

"Well, I'm frustrated because there's so much hostility."

"Of course there's hostility! You left!" Justin snapped.

Dr. Anderson intervened. "Let's talk about where we go from here. The fact is, you're separated, and Justin, you've indicated to me that this isn't working for you. You need to have some certainty as to where things are going, but I know Christi can't give you that certainty right now."

Then he suggested that we continue the separation and set a time frame for when a decision would be made. "How much time apart do you think you need before you can have a clearer picture?" he asked us.

We both just sat there like children in a time-out. We didn't say a word because we didn't have a clue.

"Okay. How about one month?" he asked. "Does that sound good?"

Justin shrugged his shoulders. "I guess so."

I, on the other hand, caved. I felt like I just needed out. I wanted some closure. But I heard the word *okay* come out of my mouth.

As Dr. Anderson and Justin talked about what this separation would mean, my head was screaming, *No! No! Let's just get this over with!* Even so, I couldn't bring myself to say the word *divorce*. I was afraid of hurting Justin even more. And I was still dealing with the guilt I felt over leaving. Dr. Anderson's words echoed in my ears. I had to be patient here. I had to give Justin time to get used to the idea of our not being together.

Justin looked at me. "How do you even feel, Christi? Where's your head?"

"I have to admit I'm not hopeful at this point. I do love you, but I just can't live with all the tumult and belittling anymore."

At that point Dr. Anderson stepped in to mediate. "Okay, we have to set some ground rules. Justin, it's clear Christi needs some space. If you really want to salvage this marriage, you need to let her be. Let's agree to just a few conversations a week and limit them to business—finances, insurance, work issues. But no heavy conversations about where your relationship is headed."

We both agreed. We also agreed to keep our separation quiet and not announce it to our friends and work colleagues. Justin didn't want to deal with the scrutiny, and since we worked opposite hours, it wouldn't be that difficult to pull it off. Although my head was screaming to let it all out, I relented.

I felt like I'd spent so much time living a lie. I didn't want to lie to anyone anymore! I didn't think there was any chance for reconciliation—though I'll admit there was a razor-thin sliver of me that was watching him, wondering if he'd make any real effort to remedy this. And when I stepped back, I could see Justin's perspective on wanting to keep it quiet. In the end, there were a few select people who knew—people I could count on to listen to me and give me advice. I had to be content with that for now.

———•———

The restrictions Dr. Anderson put on my communication with Justin didn't really help matters. Justin was calling me regularly, arguing about money and asking why it was taking me so long to make up my mind. He kept telling me, "I don't know how long I can take this, Christi. I don't think I can last a month." I was riddled with guilt, but simultaneously exasperated. This wasn't what we'd agreed to! And during that month, I'd hoped that he would be doing some soul-searching of his own.

There was something else about his words that struck me. In all our conversations, I never once heard him say, "I want you back. I want this to work out. I'll do whatever it takes." And certainly his actions weren't communicating to me that he was willing to do whatever it took. A few times when he called me, it was apparent from his slurred speech and malicious tone that he'd been drinking. These conversations only reinforced to me that there was no way I could go back to him—not if he couldn't face his alcohol issues and agree to the terms we'd set up, even for a month.

The day after our session with Dr. Anderson, I was turning the key to my new town house. It was in a gated community, which I loved for the sake of its security, and it was just the right size for me. There was even a fireplace that gave me an immediate sense of warmth and comfort.

You should have seen me! I ran around from empty room to empty room, jumping up and down like an immature teenager. I laughed at myself.

There I was, with no furniture, no television—not even phone service yet. I had nothing but my own air to breathe. But that was enough.

Over the course of the next couple of weeks, I purchased some furniture and met with Dr. Anderson a few times, once with Justin there. I told him I'd gotten my own place, and we started talking about what to divvy up. Although we still had a couple of weeks before we'd sit down and face the divorce decision head-on, there were a few things at our apartment that I wanted to pick up: the rest of my clothes, some books, and some dishes. We agreed I'd get them while Justin was at work.

It was cloudy and chilly the next afternoon when I walked up the steps to our apartment. When I walked in, I felt like a visitor. I suppose I was. It wasn't my place anymore. It felt cold and foreign. Memories of the threats, the yelling, and the crying seemed to hang in the air. If those walls could talk, they'd tell a story I'd never want to relive.

I got to work making trips from the closet to the car, then moved my way to the kitchen. I took a painting off the wall that I'd worked on a couple of years ago. Next I took down a picture my aunt had given me of Lakeside, a little community on Lake Erie. My family had had a cottage there for as long as I could remember, and we'd spend time there every summer. I had fond memories of playing shuffleboard and putt-putt and swimming in the lake.

There was one particularly memorable night when my friends and I were jumping off the dock during a huge thunderstorm. Our fun was interrupted when a police officer came and ordered all of us out of the water. We thought we were such rebels! We had no idea how tuned in Gram was to everything that happened there until the next morning. When we woke up, she said casually, "So, I hear the police had to haul some kids out of the water during the thunderstorm last night." She didn't even look up from her paper. It was just her way of saying, "I know what you did, and don't do it again."

I stood in our living room, staring at the picture of the Lakeside dock. It was taken in the evening, just after the sun had set. The dark blue sky in the background was illuminated by lights that were strung along a white Adirondack chair.

Isn't it funny how one picture can give you so much comfort? The image took me back to a time when things were simpler, more secure. It was a reminder of how beautiful this world can be.

I packed up the picture with the rest of my things, knowing it didn't mean much to Justin. He probably wouldn't even notice it was gone.

I grabbed half of the dishes in the kitchen. I'm not kidding. I stood at the counter and literally counted six of everything—six plates, six forks, six spoons, six glasses. I didn't want to be accused of taking too much or being unfair to him. I left the china and crystal untouched. I knew that was something that would have to be negotiated. I looked at the clock and realized I'd been there for two hours. Justin could be coming home any minute. I scurried out with my arms full of one last load and hopped in the car.

By the time I pulled out of the parking lot, drops of rain had started pelting the windshield. As I looked at these belongings piled up in my little car, everything felt odd. I couldn't decide if the pouring rain was cleansing or if it was a dark reminder of how sad this situation was. I felt guilty when I imagined Justin walking into our closet and seeing it half-empty. Would it be the jolt he needed to make the necessary changes in his life? Would he finally face what he needed to face? Or would it just enrage him?

The whole drive home, I was enveloped in an ominous cloud. I didn't feel guilty for leaving him. I knew that had to be. But I did feel guilty for hurting him.

Twenty-five minutes later I pulled up to the gate of my new complex, and I felt like my life was in front of me now, just waiting for me to grab it and run with it. I parked in the garage and started taking armfuls of things into the town house. This would be my first night there since I'd left. I locked the door tight behind me. As far as I knew, Justin wasn't aware of my location.

I walked into the bedroom and looked at my new bedroom furniture. My first solo purchase. It was exactly what I'd always wanted—but it was bare. It was nothing fancy—just a set of sheets and two pillows. No comforter to dress it up. No big pillows to sink into. It was as plain as could be. But it was mine. I smiled, ran toward the bed, and took a flying leap onto the mattress. Then I spread out on my back, as if I were getting ready to make a snow angel.

After a couple of minutes I walked around the house and envisioned how in time I'd make it my own. Right now it was empty—no furniture, nothing on the walls. But eventually I'd hang pictures, find candles for the mantel, buy a new coffee table, and get a bed for the guest room. For once the silence and emptiness didn't feel lonely; it felt peaceful. I didn't care that I had nothing else to my name at the moment. I was standing in my own place, truly on my own for the first time in a long time.

And it already felt like home.

After organizing the kitchen and talking to Nanette and Jen on my cell phone, I crawled into bed around 11 p.m. I lay there looking out the glass doors that led to the patio. It was almost completely dark, but I could make out the bougainvilleas climbing along the wall. I breathed in and exhaled big. What was most beautiful was that I felt no fear. No fear that Justin would come in late and rip the covers off me, screaming. No fear that he'd hurt me. No fear of his tirades or accusations. I closed my eyes and fell into a restful sleep.

For about thirty minutes.

That's when Justin called my cell phone, enraged at what I'd taken from the apartment. He said he knew I was taking clothes and some dishes but not pictures off the wall. I told him I was sorry, but the two pictures I had taken had no sentimental meaning to him that I knew of, so I didn't think it would matter to him. Then he started pushing me for an answer about what I wanted to do. Did I want a divorce?

"I don't know how long I can do this, Christi. I don't want a divorce, but I can't handle this."

It was the first time since I'd left that he said he didn't want a divorce. But he still wasn't telling me he'd do whatever it took to make sure that didn't happen. He didn't take any responsibility for his anger or addiction. I never heard him say, "I'm sorry."

"Let's just give it the time Dr. Anderson suggested, and we'll go from there," I said.

We met with Dr. Anderson the next day and discussed furniture. We agreed that I'd take the second TV, the one that had been mine when we got together, as well as one of the couches and the small dining table that was a family antique. It had been my grandmother's, then my parents', then mine. I was surprised at how agreeable Justin was about everything.

A couple of days later I was standing on the porch of what was now solely Justin's apartment. The moving guys came and took the couch, TV, and dining set. Justin and I actually laughed and joked around a bit. There were still some things to go through, but we could do that later. I left feeling really good.

For as volatile as things could get between Justin and me, we also had some really good times together. He had a quick wit and sharp mind, and I liked to engage that side of him. I held him in high esteem for his thoughts on current events and the news biz. It was refreshing to have a meeting that wasn't characterized by animosity or arguing.

That night I was sitting alone at home feeling—for lack of a better word—funky. As happy as I was to be on my own, I was beginning to absorb the gravity of what was happening. And it was sad. That was the only word to describe it. Sad that it had to come to this. Sad that Justin was hurting and that the good parts of what we had were crumbling right in front of us. The positive times we had together, like earlier that day, only amplified the sadness over what was left.

What was blatantly clear to me, however, was that I was sad because of *how* it ended, not sad *because* it ended. There's a big difference. No part of me wanted to go back to Justin. It was glorious to wake up each morning without the fear of being judged or criticized or ridiculed. From the moment I got up each day, my feet were planted firmly on the floor, no longer tiptoeing around, trying to avoid the land mines that could blow up in my face if I said or did the wrong thing.

People often think holding on is what makes you strong, but sometimes it's letting go. I was committed to releasing all that haunted me from this relationship. I wanted to learn from it, yes, but I was no longer willing to be chained to the memories that made me feel inadequate, insecure, and fearful.

That night I ate dinner, went for a run, and then simply forced myself to sit there in silence. No television. No phone. No music.

I imposed upon myself brutal honesty. It seemed the only way to go. If I'd been living in a bubble, then it was time to burst it.

People often think holding on is what makes you strong, but sometimes it's letting go.

Justin and I were just days away from the one-month mark. Before I told Justin I wanted a divorce, there were four questions I really needed to answer. I wanted to make sure I left this situation with integrity and with as little emotional baggage as possible. That was the only way to move ahead. None of us can go through an abusive relationship without taking scars with us when we leave. A Band-Aid isn't the answer. We need to clean out those wounds and apply healing ointment to them.

So I wrote down these four questions:

1. Why did I marry him?
2. Why did I leave him?
3. Why did I allow myself to put up with the abuse?
4. What did I want now?

I started off by tackling number one: why did I marry Justin? First, I loved him. That was true, and the answer came easily.

At one time I'd loved him very much. In the beginning he was thoughtful and kind. He made me feel like he was always thinking about me and that he valued his time with me. And there were moments during our marriage when I still felt that.

But once the abuse started—the name-calling, the vulgar language, the punching of walls, the accusations of infidelity, the drinking, and the lying—it superseded those times of connection between us. My fear became more prevalent than those sweet moments.

I had to be truthful with myself, though. I had also married Justin out of fear, which was ironic because that was also why I'd left him. I was afraid that if I didn't go to Boise with him, I'd lose him.

Oh, how pathetic! I thought as I came face-to-face with that reality. *Was I really that stupid?*

But wait, no more name-calling. I was learning to differentiate my own voice from Justin's. I'd been through enough of that already.

Okay, deep breath. Keep going.

I thought back to that time when I decided to marry Justin instead of going to Cleveland. I feared letting him go, because— wait for it—what if he were my last chance at happiness? What if he was "the one" and one day I'd end up alone, regretting not marrying him?

Okay, so it *was* pretty pathetic.

I was twenty-seven years old at the time. Most of my friends were already married, so I suppose I felt like I had some catching up to do. I had to ask myself, *Did I marry him just because I wanted to get married?*

I sat on that a long time. I considered it fully. I didn't want to be alone, and that was definitely a factor in my decision. I needed to own my codependency issues. But ultimately that wasn't the whole story.

I allowed my mind and my heart to go back in time to when Justin gave me the ultimatum of going to Cleveland without him or going to Boise with him. What did I see in him that held me to him?

I swallowed hard. The truth is, we're often attracted to people who have something we desire for ourselves.

I wanted to marry Justin because he seemed so self-assertive and brave and sturdy to me at a time when I was feeling especially vulnerable. I saw in him something I wanted to be: strong.

Most of us sense a void inside us that nothing else seems to fill. So when we see what we lack in someone else, we cling to it as if our lives depended on it.

We can have heroes in this life, but we can only have one Savior. That God-shaped hole won't be filled by anything less than God Himself.

Now, this isn't entirely a bad thing—our differences can complement each other, no doubt. But we can never live vicariously through another person. We need to find our wholeness, our sense of completion on our own. No human will be able to do that for us.

Besides, that's a lot of pressure to put on someone. Even if they don't realize the expectation, on some level, they probably feel it. Sure, we can have heroes in this life, but we can only have one Savior. That God-shaped hole won't be filled by anything less than God Himself.

I realized now that when I said yes to Justin, I was in no frame of mind to make that kind of decision. At the time I was living with a massive hollow, and I tried to fill it with a man. That wasn't fair to either of us.

So . . . I married Justin because (1) I loved him, (2) I feared being without him, (3) I had some codependency issues, and (4) I saw a strength in him that I wanted for myself.

Okay. Good start.

What I knew, too, was that marrying him was my choice. This was a fact I couldn't ignore.

I couldn't blame Justin for giving me an ultimatum. I couldn't put it on P.A.'s death and the ache it left in me. Regardless of my reasons, I chose to marry him, and I had to own that. It wasn't his fault or anyone else's.

That led me down another path: was this relationship a mistake? I didn't think so. Every relationship, every meeting with another person, gives us a chance to learn something. God can use each interaction to open us up to more of who we are. And that's not a mistake.

I was finally starting to realize that those years spent locked in this turmoil helped me find a strength I might never have found had it not been for this relationship. I discovered a whole new level of independence, courage, faith, and conviction. And what's interesting, too, is that this experience gave me the freedom to accept people just as they are. Without evaluating them or sizing them up. I knew what it was like to live in someone else's prison, and I wasn't about to impose that on anyone else.

So as I sat there thinking about not just who I was but who

I wanted to be, I released the blame I was feeling toward myself. And I prayed for forgiveness, mercy, and guidance.

I was already starting to feel stronger, like I had a better grasp on who I was. But there was still so much to explore.

It would have to wait. I was exhausted, and I wanted to bask in this feeling of clarity.

I crawled into my bed—alone but happy.

CHAPTER 12

DON'T LET YESTERDAY
WASTE TODAY

WHILE JUSTIN AND I had agreed to keep the separation under the radar, I knew he'd told a few of his friends what was happening. I hoped it was helping him. There were days I needed support too. My family was there for me, of course, but I needed someone who was close to me in heart and in proximity. My sweet friend Sam, who was also my co-anchor, became another go-to person for me.

When O'Neill and Phil had hired me, they created the co-anchor position to fit me onto their team. As excited as I was for the opportunity, I had some trepidations. Let's be honest—we all know that women can be downright mean to each other at times, especially if they feel their territory is threatened. While I didn't see myself as a threat, I wasn't really sure how I'd be received. For all I knew, Sam was saying to herself, *Who does this little chick think she is, invading my show?* So I did my best to tread lightly.

This business, like many others, is full of egos. I had seen the damage done as a result of inflated self-images in the past, so I was committed to keeping my ego in check. I never wanted to get too big for my britches or act like someone couldn't get along without me. I was well aware that while I was capable at doing my job, it wasn't my entire identity. But when it came to what kind of reception I'd receive from my coworker, I wasn't sure what to expect.

I quickly learned, however, that my concerns couldn't have been more off base. Sam immediately reached out to me with her generous spirit and kind heart, and we were a team from the get-go. They gave us a lot of freedom on the show, and shortly after my arrival, we partnered with the Arizona Humane Society. I started a segment called "Sunday's Sweetheart," which featured a different pet each week in need of a good home. Shortly before Justin and I separated, the spokeswoman for the humane society told me our segment was one of their most successful placement programs. In fact, every animal we'd featured thus far had been adopted. My heart swelled when I heard that. At such a low point of my life, it was meaningful to feel like I was contributing to some positive change.

This was also about the time Phil called Sam and me in to talk about ratings. We started throwing ideas at him about what we'd like to do to improve the show (we had four hours to fill, after all), but he stopped us. "Hold on!" he said. "I'm not prepared to add any more resources to the show. I just wanted to tell you nice job. "

Then he showed us the ratings. We were the number one show on weekend mornings against all the other network affiliates. Sam and I looked at each other, and we were simply grateful. We had no illusions this was all about us, but we appreciated the fact that the newscast had become even more than Phil had expected. It was a nice boost to my confidence at this tumultuous time. And it was nice knowing I was working with a woman I could trust. We had each other's backs. That had been true from the start—personally and professionally.

But while Sam knew things were dicey for me at home, she didn't realize how much the situation had escalated. Shortly after Justin and I separated, I told her in confidence what was happening and that I was planning to file for divorce. I'll never forget the look of sadness on her face.

"Oh, no! Christi, I'm so sorry! What can I do?"

Sam is a woman of faith. Her comforting support helped hold me up many a day, and her words of wisdom were invigorating. As Sam said, this wasn't the end of my world; it was actually the beginning.

As it turned out, I would need her encouragement more than I imagined. Things were about to get ugly.

—— •— ——

I assumed that once Justin and I were separated, I would feel safe. And while that was true to some extent, I hadn't counted on the fact that abuse doesn't just show up in person. It can come over the phone, in letters, via e-mail, and nowadays through social media. And some evenings, the phone was not my friend.

The ring would startle me awake in the middle of the night, and I'd pick up to hear Justin railing at me. During one particularly heated conversation, he again accused me of cheating on him. But this time he got specific. He came up with some outrageous story about how Eric, an old boyfriend from high school, had left a message for me, saying he really needed to talk to me and that it was urgent.

Justin growled, "I hope you had a good time screwing him when you were home!"

"What are you talking about?" I cried. "I don't even know where he lives or what he's doing!" I hadn't seen Eric in years.

Justin went on to accuse and berate me, not even giving me a chance to defend myself. He was irrational and talking in circles. I was quite certain he'd been drinking.

I knew he'd concocted the story, so I asked him to play the message for me.

"Oh, I accidentally erased it," he said.

Only two minutes before, he told me he'd just gotten home and called me immediately after he heard it. Things weren't adding up. Unless someone called and left a message over the old one, the original message wouldn't be erased. Not to mention the fact that Eric didn't have my number—and was happily married.

"I'm sure while you were home you had a great time in bed with him, and I'll bet Nanette couldn't be happier!" he hissed.

I actually laughed at this point because it proved how little this man knew about me—this man I'd been married to for four years. It was true that I had been engaged to Nanette's brother at one point. But her brother was Scott. Yes, that man I'd met in college, not high school.

And incidentally, Scott, too, was now happily married.

I finally hung up on Justin and spent the rest of the evening kicking myself for allowing him to talk to me like that again. *Why do I give him the opportunity?*

I read somewhere that in order to be walked on, you have to be lying down. Well, I wasn't going to lie down any longer.

I knew in that moment that I had to find the power God had given me. And I had to learn not just to stand in it but to stand tall.

The next morning I got the chance when Justin called.

He started in, as usual, but this time I'd had it. Before long we were screaming at each other.

"Your anger is out of control!" I told him. "Even if Eric did call, I have no control over that. I haven't seen or talked to him in more than four years. And here's a bombshell for you—Nanette doesn't even know Eric! He's not her brother! I think you've created this scenario about *In order to be walked on, you have to be lying down.* me supposedly sleeping with him and had the gall to go ballistic about something completely fabricated. Do you realize this is why I left?"

He yelled back, "I know somebody put this idea of divorce in your head, Christi!"

I was livid. Now Justin was accusing Nanette, and I couldn't hold my tongue. I knew the truth, and I wasn't afraid to say it.

"Yes, that's true. You know who it was? It was *you*, Justin! Every time you got mad, you threatened to leave. You told me you never wanted to see me again unless it was in divorce court. You told me you were sorry you ever married me! So if you want someone to blame for putting that idea in my head, look in the mirror!"

"I can't take this anymore!" he shouted back. "Is this what you want? A divorce? Because I can't hang in here much longer!"

I couldn't tell if he was spouting the words from sheer fury or if he was methodically choosing his verbiage. Whenever he said things like "I can't hang in here much longer," it frightened me because I wondered if he'd do something to harm himself. I didn't know if it was his way of scaring me or if there was some truth to what he was saying. Either way, it really messed with my head.

The next morning I was in Dr. Anderson's office for an already-scheduled appointment. I was a wreck.

Dr. Anderson had had a couple of sessions with Justin recently, and although I knew he couldn't tell me specifics due to client confidentiality, I wanted to hear his perspective.

It wasn't promising.

After I relayed my latest conversation with Justin to Dr. Anderson, he looked right at me. "Christi," he said, "I'm concerned that Justin isn't really dealing with things the way I hoped he would. He seems more concerned about how this is affecting him than about his own part in the separation. I haven't heard him say, 'I know I've screwed up.' I haven't seen him take any responsibility."

Oh, thank you, God! I said silently. In a strange way, it was a relief to hear Dr. Anderson say that. It meant someone else was observing the same thing I'd been witnessing for years. But I was so close to the situation I didn't trust myself to make an unbiased assessment of Justin's behavior. Now a professional was coming to the same conclusion I'd suspected.

"What do I do now?" I asked. "I don't think Justin is capable of changing until he realizes his part in this. And honestly, I don't know that it's ever going to happen."

Dr. Anderson paused and folded his hands together. Then he leaned back in his chair. "You know, the way someone has acted in the past can give us great insight into what kind of future to expect with them. I think this is one of those instances."

Yeah. Me too.

It's like Oprah says: "When people show you who they are, believe them." And while Justin had his strong points, he certainly hadn't admitted to his drinking, his abuse, or any role he played in this mess.

What was frightening to me, as I thought about all this, was that maybe he didn't even realize he'd been abusive. What if he thought the words he spewed at me were justified or normal? Or that he was somehow entitled to his tantrums? If this was the case, there would be no chance of turning this relationship around.

And I had to be honest about myself, too. I knew that if I opened myself to him again, if I held on to hope and let him hurt me one more time, I was going to crack. I was literally going to crumble emotionally until there was nothing of the real me left.

I wasn't willing to go to that place again.

After talking with Dr. Anderson, I knew for sure that divorce was the only option. It was time to let go of the thin thread of hope I'd been hanging on to that Justin still might be willing to change, that our marriage could still be salvaged. The thread had snapped. There was nothing left to save.

But first I needed to return to the four questions I had started to answer.

I went home, sat down by myself, and fiercely searched for honesty in question number two.

Why did I leave Justin?

One, while I still loved him as a person, I wasn't in love with him anymore. Now, I firmly believe that in some circumstances, love can be rekindled after it's been lost. All couples go through seasons of closeness or routine. But with this kind of denial going on, this kind of lying and viciousness, I saw no chance that trust and closeness could be resuscitated.

Two, I left him because I had finally started to love myself again. I'd heard so many threats, been called so many vulgar names, that I'd lost respect for myself. I thought I had no worth, no right to happiness.

But somewhere along this journey, I remembered my roots, which brought me back to remembering who I was, who I'd always wanted to be. And that discovery pushed me closer to God. I knew I didn't have all the answers, but I was starting to trust again. Trust God. Trust myself. Trust that there was a plan and purpose hidden behind this madness. I believed that in His timing, God would reveal what I needed to do next.

His timing. Ugh! That was the daunting part. The whole waiting thing again.

I was so used to being on a deadline at work and rushing to get things done. And with all the technology at our fingertips, we get used to instantaneous answers. That sense of immediacy melds into every aspect of our lives. We have to learn the discipline of slowing down.

And so I forced myself to say, "Okay, God, I don't know what to do. The only thing I can do is nothing for now. I'll let you disclose it to me . . . in Your timing."

I was finally coming to a place of trusting that God would take care of me.

The third reason I left Justin was because I knew I would break if I didn't. This wasn't just about making a better life for myself; this was about survival.

I reflected on those years of searching for answers and feeling as though I literally wanted to die rather than live the way I was living. But somewhere in the midst of that internal chaos, I had the wherewithal to know that wasn't the kind of life God put any of us on this earth for. I knew I had a purpose, and I had to choose. Life or death? Truth or a lie?

By the grace of God, I found the strength to choose life. And truth.

Had I stayed, it would have surely killed me. If not physically, it would have murdered my soul. And that's no way for anyone to live.

Number four, I left because I couldn't bring children into a relationship like that. Having a family had been a dream of mine for as long as I could remember, and I loved my children beyond words, before they were even born. There was no way I could introduce precious, innocent children into a home filled with such volatility and enmity. How could I shield them from the outbursts and destructiveness? I couldn't count on Justin to give children security and a sense of stability when even I didn't have that with him. And how could I have prepared my children for the real world when I was tiptoeing through my day in a mode of constant defense?

I believe that home should be a sanctuary. A place where you're always accepted, always safe. Not a place of fear. I believe the saying holds true: "If a child doesn't learn love at home, she will rarely learn it somewhere else."

My home with Justin was none of the things I'd pictured a home, or a marriage, to be. And it certainly wasn't a place I'd want my precious children calling home.

Then came my fifth reason: I left because there was no hope things were going to get better.

Again, I heard the words of Justin's dad echoing in my ear: "Alcoholism is a disease, Christi. It's like cancer. You can't choose not to have it."

Okay. So choose differently.

I thought about people who do have cancer and the incredible injustice of it all, the pain they experience—both physical and emotional. And yet, as I've attended many a breast cancer walk, I've seen some of the most beautiful, vibrant, bald women laughing and walking and hugging. Women who refuse to be defined by their disease.

Yes, there is great injustice in disease. But there is also choice. If people are victims of disease, they can choose to be bitter and angry. They can choose to shut out the people who love them or lash out at the world. They can choose to shrivel up and die.

Or they can choose to live each day as if it's their last—loving the people close to them, forgiving what needs to be forgiven, inspiring people they don't even know with their strength of spirit.

I'll never forget a woman our newscast once profiled for a story. She was a mom of four young kids, and she'd been married to her high school sweetheart for years. After her diagnosis, the family's sole purpose became keeping her alive. I recognized her from our story when I ran into her at a health food store one day. She was truly glowing from the inside out. She didn't have a lot of energy, but she exuded an extraordinary sort of kindness and grace that's unmistakable. I will never forget her. She gave me hope.

The day Carey and I went to her funeral was excruciating. I grieved as I watched her children and husband mourn this woman who had been the backbone of their family. Yet I was awed by how graciously she'd prepared her children for this day with her personal letters and songs—and most of all, her peace. She made sure they knew that her love would never leave them, that she'd see them again, and that as much as she'd miss them, she was looking forward to seeing her God on the other side.

I would never apologize for not being someone's emotional punching bag. That was not my job. Not my destiny. It's not yours either—or anyone else's.

She was gone, but her legacy lingered with all of us who were there.

Justin, in contrast, seemed to be choosing denial, not change. It was the same choice he had been making for four years. And let's face it—so had I. But not anymore.

I had given him so many chances to say, "I have a disease, and I can't do this without you." Or forget "I can't do this without you"—I'd even have taken the "I have a disease" part! At the very least, a simple "I'm sorry" would have gone a long way. Any glimmer of hope that he got it—that he was willing to make a genuine effort to face problems head-on—would have been enough for me to keep fighting for our marriage.

But no. I didn't get any of that.

So I left. Did I feel sad for him? Yes. Was I angry at him? Yes.

But he had made his choice, and I'd made mine. We are responsible for our own decisions. Period.

And of all the things I was sorry for, I would never apologize for not being willing to continue living that life. I would never apologize for not being someone's emotional punching bag. That was not my job. Not my destiny. It's not anyone's.

I used to think there was some guarantee that when you got married you'd never be alone. You'd always have someone to count on. Sure, there would be obstacles and challenges, but you'd go through them together.

As I sat in my home alone, I had more peace, more joy, more contentment than I'd ever had living with Justin. I realized that simply being married doesn't guarantee you any of those things—especially if you're not married to the right person.

As I rewound that thought in my head, I said aloud, "Wow."

This was an awakening. And it drove me back to that first question: Why did I marry him?

I had already examined this and recognized that I was attracted to the strength, determination, and ambition in him that I felt I was lacking. But I needed to get to the core of it: *why* didn't I have those qualities? Why wasn't I okay being alone? Why did it take four years of tumult to start valuing myself—broken parts and all?

Suddenly a memory from my angst-filled teenage years popped into my head. As if it were a scene from a movie, I saw the fifteen-year-old me standing on the front porch of my house. I had just gotten home from cheerleading practice, and the leaves were starting to change color on the trees by the curb. I was getting grilled by Eric. Yes, Eric, that old boyfriend Justin had confused with my former fiancé.

He had just left school after talking to Felicia for half an hour. I was standing on the top step leading to our front door, and he was standing on the bottom step looking up at me. He was admonishing me for having, and being, "too much."

"You've got everything, Christi!" he said. "You're vice president of the class, you're on student council, you've got a ton of friends. You wonder why Felicia hates you? Give someone else a chance, will you? You don't deserve all this!"

And there it was! I gasped as it all came back to me so vividly.

I could see that was the moment when I started believing I wasn't enough. I had more than I deserved. I wasn't worthy of all the gifts I'd been given. That was when I started to accept two ugly lies that would haunt me for almost twenty years:

1. The more I had or the more I was, the more people would hate me.
2. All the good I had was too much, and I didn't deserve any of it.

My playing small didn't just start with Justin! It started years before when very real fears and insecurities began nesting inside me. As the years wore on, they became bigger and louder and more convincing, brainwashing me to believe that I didn't deserve the good people and things I had in my life.

A gigantic chunk of my confidence was zapped in that single conversation, which lingered with me for years and manifested itself in multiple ways, from my fear of not having enough savings in the bank to my fear of being alone to my fear of success. I worried that if I succeeded at something, either it would be taken away from me because I didn't deserve it or people would hate me and I'd be left alone. I suppose that's why I looked for men with those traits—the charisma, the confidence, the ambition I was lacking. And Justin seemed, at the time we met, to be one of those men.

I was discovering that being alone is okay. In fact, it's better than okay. Sometimes it's necessary.

Tears were streaming down my face by this point. This time they were tears not of sadness but of freedom. At least now I knew where some of my warped thoughts and insecurities stemmed from.

It was finally happening: the codependency I'd lived with was starting to evaporate. One by one, each layer of insecurity was peeling away.

I was discovering that being alone was okay. In fact, it was better than okay. Sometimes it was necessary.

I glanced at the list I'd made:

Why I Left Justin

1. I left because there was still too much lying and deception to heal all those broken places between us.
2. I left because I was finally learning to love and respect myself again.
3. I left because I knew that if I didn't, I was going to fall apart.
4. I left because it was such an unhealthy environment that I couldn't bring children into it.

5. I left because there was no hope that it was going to change or get better.
6. And perhaps most important, I left because I realized I'd rather be alone than be with the wrong person.

CHAPTER 13

BE STILL AND KNOW

THE NEXT EVENING I sat in the stillness of my bedroom, listening. I'd heard a song the other day that said, "In the quiet, love is reaching. . . . Be still and know."

I prayed, "God, am I doing the right thing?"

Silence.

Then I heard something, although the words weren't audible. *Never fear. I have much planned for you, and you will serve me much better in another place.*

Was this in my head, or was this God? I started to talk out loud, just saying whatever was on my mind.

"I know I'm not my best with Justin."

More silence. Then I sensed this response: *Joys are unfolding. You will be loved.*

Okay, I still didn't know if this was my subconscious or God Himself, but I felt a calmness come over me, washing away my anxiety. I could only do what was in my power to do. I couldn't control how Justin would react, and I couldn't change the fact that leaving felt like the first thing I'd done right in a long time.

Those last words brought peace, but they also brought some questions. Loved by whom? And how could I trust that I'd be able to recognize that love when it arrived? After all, I hadn't done such a bang-up job of that up to this point.

I felt a calmness come over me, washing away my anxiety. I could only do what was in my power to do.

But I truly felt a revival rumbling inside me. One thing I knew absolutely: if I could survive this marriage and divorce, those years of abuse, and my own insecurities, I could survive anything.

Of course I had to keep telling myself that, because it was the eve of "it." The one-month mark. The day I'd tell Justin I wanted a divorce.

That night I went to a going-away party for one of the photographers at work who was moving to Flagstaff for a new job. Everyone was laughing and joking and celebrating with her. When people asked me where Justin was, I simply said he had other plans. I didn't know what else to say. I couldn't very well blurt out, "Oh, he's not here because we're quits! Kaput! He's in my rearview mirror, and I have no idea where he spends his time these days."

At the end of the evening I walked out to my car and just stood there looking at the house. It was dark outside, and there was a cool breeze blowing. I watched everyone through the window for a moment, realizing that this was it. This was the last night anyone would look at me as Mrs. Justin Barnes. The last night anyone would connect me to him as his wife, as opposed to his ex-wife. The last night I'd be seen as part of a couple. After that night I'd have a whole new persona to those coworkers—and even to myself.

That's one of the hardest parts of a breakup. You're used to being seen as part of a couple. It has been part of your identity all this time, and suddenly the way you look to other people—and the way you look to yourself—changes. It's hard to reconcile the person you were with the person you've become.

We think we have a good picture of who we are. But then, when we're standing in that picture all by ourselves rather than beside someone else, it feels lonely.

But sometimes that's just how it has to be.

I got in my car, and as I drove away, there it was again. The stinging in my eyes. The rush in my chest. The gush of tears.

I didn't have an ounce of doubt about what needed to happen the next day. And in my gut I was sure Justin knew what was coming. But as I drove away from the gathering, I realized something else that was going to be torturous: telling everyone else.

We think we have a good picture of who we are. But then, when we're standing in that picture all by ourselves rather than beside someone else, it feels lonely.

Would people be shocked? Would they think I was a horrible person? Would they take sides? Team Justin vs. Team Christi? I could already hear the whispers, the speculations, the criticisms.

I took a deep breath. *Hold on, Christi. You don't know how anyone will react. And you don't know that everyone will blame you just because Justin does.*

"God, please help me say the right words tomorrow," I whispered aloud. "Please let Justin accept my decision with peace. And help him reach out to Dr. Anderson to make it through this. And please forgive me."

I'd been selfish at times. I'd been angry. And I'd built up a wall that Justin probably would have needed a bulldozer to barrel through. But I knew one thing for sure: I had really tried. I had given this marriage all I had for as long as I could. I had exhausted every resource available in an attempt to remedy our issues. That gave me assurance as I followed through on this heartbreaking decision.

When I got home, I remembered an assignment Colleen had given me in a recent e-mail. She told me, "Write a letter to yourself from God. Imagine what words God would say to guide you through this whole mess. You might be surprised at what you find."

It was a bizarre concept to me, but on the eve of declaring my divorce official, what did I have to lose?

So I sat down and started typing.

Dear Christi,

I am with you. You're not alone. I've been with you the entire journey, and I'll be beside you every step of the future. And I'll be with Justin, too. I won't abandon him, and I'll help him in ways you simply cannot. I know this has been torture for both of you. I know how guilty you feel for hurting him, and I know all about his pain too.

But there are better days ahead. I promise. Don't think I haven't seen what has been happening. I want to assure you it's not going to end this way, though. I know it's frightening, but My hand is on your shoulder and My voice is in your heart. You've done everything you can to fix this. You have to trust that I know what's best for you both, even if you don't.

Put your faith and trust in Me, dear child. You are My child. And My love for you and Justin exceeds all you could ever imagine. I'll never leave you. Go forward in strength and courage. Keep your eyes on Me, and I'll lead the way. We're in this together. We always will be.

I love you.

God

I think I finished the letter in five minutes. There was one thing in particular that struck me when I reread it: I couldn't believe how much compassion and love exuded from the words. It had to be God's voice, because it was an entirely different tone from what I heard when I talked to myself.

When our inner voice speaks up, we often hear words laced with cynicism, admonishment, and shame. But when we get quiet, when we choose to be still, the verbiage changes to a firm but gentle instruction. The tone is caressed with tenderheartedness, understanding, and promise. Hope punctuates each sentence. Empathy seeps from every phrase into our weary souls. The words are gentle, but they are powerful enough to move our spirits. To soothe our wounds. To reshape our warped visions.

It was jolting to consider the disparity between the words Justin used toward me and the words contained in that letter. In the last four years, the words that had moved me were ones that moved me to tears and anger. I didn't want to do that to anyone else. I wanted to be firm in what I said but still communicate in a considerate, thoughtful way. I was learning that sometimes the gentlest words have the most power, and I was eager to put that lesson into practice.

I knew that tomorrow I was going to get that chance.

———•——

The next morning my phone rang early.

"Christi? It's Anna," Justin's mom said.

After a few pleasantries, we got down to the nitty-gritty.

"We're just wondering if you can let us know what you plan to do today so we can be prepared," she said.

I took a deep breath. "Anna, I love Justin, but I just can't take this volatility anymore. I can't live like this." My throat started to close up, and my voice was trembling now as tears started streaming down my cheeks. I couldn't disguise my angst.

"I'm just so, so sorry," I whispered. It was all I could get out.

I heard her sigh. "Christi, you're the daughter I never had. . . ." Her voice cracked. "I know you've tried very hard to make this work."

"I wish I could have done more."

"Well, Justin is expecting to hear that you're going to ask for a divorce. In fact, he'll be heading home tomorrow to spend some time with us so we can work through it all."

A wave of relief swept through me.

"I'm so glad to hear that. He'll listen to you and Dad. It will mean so much that you're there for him."

There was an awkward pause. I knew we had to hang up.

What made it so hard was that I knew that very well might be the last time I spoke with her. I mean, when you get divorced, I don't think you get to "keep" your in-laws, do you?

"I love you, Mom, and I'm so grateful for everything you and Mark have done for us," I said. "Thank you. You always made me feel like a real part of the family. I know this has been hard on all of you, too. Please give Mark and Jeff my love."

"I love you, too, Christi." I could tell she was crying too.

And with one more good-bye, it was over.

I sat on the couch and bawled like a baby.

Here I was crying, not only over what was to happen in a few hours, but also for the loss of Anna, Mark, and Justin's whole family.

At the same time, I finally felt understood. To hear Anna say, "I know you've tried"—she'll never know how healing those words were for me. Whether Justin or Mark or anyone else ever understands that I really gave this all I had, at least I know that she knew. She acknowledged it. And it was like medicine to my soul.

The meeting with Dr. Anderson lasted about two minutes. At least for me.

I was sitting in the office lobby when Justin walked in. He didn't even look at me. He was trying to be stoic, but I could see the anger boiling under the surface. He knew what was coming.

At that moment the fear and guilt over what I was about to do flooded me, and I started shaking. It was uncontrollable—my hands trembled, and the muscles in my whole body tensed up.

Not enough for him to notice, but I certainly knew the feeling. It was the same fear, the same physical reaction I had whenever he came home drunk.

Dr. Anderson called us into his office. I sat on one couch, and Justin sat on the other. Dr. Anderson started the meeting.

"Christi, what would you like to say?"

I inhaled, and as tears started rolling down my face, I looked at the floor. "I want to move forward with a divorce."

Silence.

I looked up at Justin, who was staring ahead, his hands clasped together in his lap.

"Justin, I'm so sorry," I offered.

He looked at me, robotic, empty. "You had your hour with Dr. Anderson a few days ago," he said. "I'd like my hour now."

I looked at Dr. Anderson and he nodded his head. "We'll talk later," he told me.

I walked out to my car, and the moment I shut the door, I started sobbing. Right there in the parking lot. I was blubbering so hard I could hardly get a breath between sobs.

My heart ached for him. I wasn't crying because it was over. I was crying because what I'd just said pierced Justin with a pain I knew all too well, and it was killing me that I was responsible for it. I'd been in the place he was in right then. I'd known what it was like to have my spouse not want me. Only this time it was official. And I was the one saying it.

"God, please be with him," I pleaded. "Give him peace and comfort." I didn't know what else to say. I prayed that same prayer all the way home.

CHAPTER 14

YOU NEVER RUN OUT OF CHANCES WITH GOD

THE NEXT MORNING as the sun gently woke me up, I opened my eyes and just lay there. I looked out the window and saw the bougainvilleas flitting in the faint breeze. And all at once I realized something: it was a new day. A new day in every sense.

"Thank you, God," I whispered. "Please be with him."

I wondered if Justin was at the airport or already on the flight to his parents' home. I pictured him staring out the window of the plane, like I'd done on my flight back from Chicago when I started feeling the weight of what was happening. The weight of the end. I wondered if that reality was hitting him now too.

"God, be with Anna and Mark. Help them help him," I prayed. I inhaled a huge breath of air until my lungs couldn't take in anymore. Then I let it all out slowly and steadily. I sat up, put my feet on the floor, and smiled.

No eggshells. Just solid floor.

I was free, and I didn't need a signed piece of paper to tell me so. That feeling of liberty was as exhilarating as if I'd just been released from prison.

It was comforting to know that Justin was surrounded by his family. I knew they'd take good care of him.

I got dressed and stepped outside into the autumn sunshine. I relished the lightness I felt as I jogged along the golf course, with the gorgeous view of Camelback Mountain straight ahead. Somehow the air felt fresher, clearer, more brilliant than it had the day before. But mostly it was my thoughts that I noticed. The heaviness I'd felt trapped under these last few months was noticeably absent. I had hope again. Hope that felt so real it might as well have been running alongside me.

I got home, showered, and then made a phone call I'd been wanting to make since we moved to Phoenix. My friend from the humane society answered, and I said, "I'm ready! Bring me my new dog!"

She asked what kind of dog to be on the lookout for.

"Whatever needs a good home," I said. "I don't care if it's male or female, big or small. I trust you."

One of the best things about animals is the unconditional love and affection they give you. A dog is always happy to see you. Always ready to cuddle up beside you. Always willing to sit close and listen to you gripe or cry, even if it doesn't understand you. That was something I needed at that moment, and it felt good to know I was providing a safe, loving place for an animal to live. I just couldn't wait to meet the little one.

I didn't have to wait long. Within a few weeks I was introduced to a tiny eight-week-old puppy. He was a terrier/basset hound mix, if you can imagine! Short and long with big paws and the long ears of a basset, but covered in the fur of a white terrier. One look from me and one tail wag from him, and it was decided. He was mine. I named him Bruno.

As I walked him along the golf course, I'd chuckle at how he'd always look back to make sure I was nearby when I let him off the leash to run wild. It was Bruno and me against the world! Everything was starting to feel right again.

The next day my former coworker in Flagstaff called to warn me that the word was out.

Oh boy, here we go! My body tensed up. This was the aspect of the breakup I dreaded almost as much as having to hurt Justin: other people catching wind of what had happened. And sure enough, our conversation sounded like something straight out of junior high.

"Rich called Scott, and I heard him cry, 'Oh, my God!' I knew right away they'd found out," she said.

"How bad is it?" I couldn't begin to imagine what they were saying. I knew I was the bad guy with Justin's family—would I be with everyone else, too?

I wish I didn't care what they thought. But I did.

"They were talking about how you were back on the market, and they wondered why Justin wouldn't fight for you."

My guard went up, and I wanted to jump to Justin's defense. I knew they were good guys, and I hoped they wouldn't blow this out of proportion. I didn't want Justin to be bad-mouthed.

"Don't worry, Christi. I'll do what I can to keep clearing the air," she said. "And you should know that Scott said he has too much respect for you to jump on the rumor bandwagon."

Wow. He had respect for me? It was surprising—and comforting—to hear that someone still held me in that esteem. But I was fully aware that this was just the beginning.

At work the next day our main anchor, Patti, came up to me. Apparently word travels fast. But we were in the news business, after all.

One thing I love about Patti is that she minces no words. She calls it like she sees it, and if it hurts, so be it. I'd solicited her advice numerous times about the industry and about news in general, but this time the conversation was clearly not going to be about work.

She walked over to my desk. "Can I ask you a personal question?"

"Of course," I replied.

"Are you getting divorced?"

There it was.

"Yes. I am."

Pause. "Can I tell you something?"

I shrugged. "Sure."

"Please don't take this the wrong way, but when I first met Justin . . . I just didn't get it."

"What do you mean?" I had no idea where this was going.

"Well, I never would have put the two of you together. I like Justin and everything, but I saw him as a player for some reason, and you just seemed like an odd match."

She paused for a moment. "You okay?"

I had to smile. "You know, it's weird, but I'm really doing well.

You're right. Justin and I are two very different people, and we just couldn't make it work."

And that was as far as I was going to take it. I had no desire to air any dirty laundry.

As the day wore on, I was blown away by the support I received from my coworkers. "If you need anything at all, I'm here," they'd say. "I'm so sorry for what you're going through." One person pulled me aside and said, "To be honest, this doesn't surprise me. I've watched the way he talks to you—the words he uses and the tone of his conversations—and I knew this wasn't a good place for you to be."

When your heart starts to open, so does your world.

I was dumbfounded by the kindness, and quite frankly, by the awareness people had about me and my situation. We might think we're doing a good job of hiding our turmoil, but I was learning that people were onto my farce more than I'd ever guessed.

It wasn't long before people from Boise were getting word too. (For the big business that television news is, it's actually pretty small.) My friend Jason e-mailed me, encouraging me that this was the best choice to make. "I honestly don't know how you sustained it as long as you did," he told me.

The whole week I had a constant stream of affirmation that, yes, this was the right answer. Even though by now, I didn't need anyone else to confirm it.

———•———

With each day that passed and each hand that reached out to me in kindness, my heart started to crack open just a little more.

A sliver here, an inch there. And when your heart starts to open, so does your world.

Beginning to believe in your own judgment after questioning yourself for so long is a rebirth of sorts. It takes time to rebuild that trust, and I was grateful for God's confirmations along the way. I thought about everything that had happened. The friends who told me Justin was drinking again. The way Justin initiated the conversation about separating. The guidance Dr. Anderson gave me. The time Jeff came to be with Justin, not knowing what was coming. The haven Carey gave me to stay in for a while.

In a way, even Justin's erratic, accusatory behavior was a blessing. It refuted any doubts I might have had that leaving was the best thing.

As I reflected on everything I'd gone through in the past few months, I was struck by this realization: when you give it to God, He really does take care of you. And I'm not special. He does that for all of us.

How often do I confine myself—and God—to limits I can understand? If I'd just stop trying to manipulate my life for a minute, stop believing that what's around me is all there is, I'd recognize that all those small coincidences that happen just might be God's way of revealing small miracles with His signature on them.

His promises are always there, just waiting for us to believe them. It's up to us to get a grip on ourselves and believe that anything is possible. Anything.

But let's be real. Trepidation still has a way of creeping in. When I finally made the decision to leave, I didn't question it. But I certainly questioned myself. When you hurt someone on the level I hurt Justin, that guilt doesn't just evaporate.

On the way home from work one night, I had a little conversation with God. Here's how it went: "God, You know I can be weak and question myself. Thank You for the hammering message of reinforcement You're giving me through these people. Thank You for their encouragement and generous words. I couldn't get through this without You. Please give me the desire of Your heart, and please . . . help my unbelief."

I was feeling more hope and confidence than I had in years. But I also knew I had a long way to go to make sure it stuck.

Back at home that night, I was at peace. It was the kind of peace that wouldn't dissipate when Justin came home—because he wasn't coming home. This wasn't his home. It was my home, and I was safe.

I felt ready to undertake question number three: Why did I allow myself to put up with the abuse for so long?

This was a tough one, because it meant I had to come to terms with my shortcomings. I had to forgive myself for staying in a situation like that. I knew I was like millions of women out there—I was smart, capable, and independent, but I'd become entangled in a relationship that was hurtful and unhealthy. It was humiliating to realize I had stayed for four years of my life. I thought again, *What alien took over my head and convinced me that I couldn't leave, that I just needed to deal with it?*

When it came down to it, I decided there were really four emotional handcuffs that kept me locked in.

First, I stayed because I believed marriage was sacred. I had made a vow not just to Justin but to God that I was in this for the long haul. I was committed to sticking to my word.

Reason number two: I stayed because I was afraid. I was starting to see this thread of fear and how much I was letting it rule my life.

I feared what Justin would do if I tried to leave. I feared what people would say if I left. I feared what my life would be like without him. I feared being alone.

It was baffling to me that I could simultaneously fear Justin and fear being without him. Even more bewildering was that my fear of being without him superseded my fear of his abuse—at least for a while.

The third reason I stayed was because on some level I still believed in Justin. In retrospect, I realized that while we had our troubles, we also had our good times. I could see now that when he was sweet or thoughtful or loving—and he certainly was at times—I'd cling to that and let it override the bad stuff. I knew there was a wonderful, decent man in there. So when I saw glimpses of it, I hung on for dear life.

Then it hit me—I stayed because if I didn't, if I acknowledged that Justin had serious issues, I'd also have to acknowledge that I was guilty of ignoring them. I'd have to own up to the fact that they had been evident before we got married and I'd glossed over them. I'd have to admit that I screwed up . . . from the get-go.

And this was a pivotal miss on my part. This wasn't just "Oh, I forgot to set my alarm, so I was late to the meeting" or "Well, I screwed up and gave the painter the wrong color code, and now the walls are bright orange." No, this was a colossal foul-up. The stakes were the lives of at least two people, and now we were left with a lot of pulverized emotions scattered all over the floor.

I never wanted to be part of this sorority of divorce. Doesn't divorce mean failure? In part at least, I stayed because I couldn't face my own failure.

God, I prayed silently, *how do I forgive myself?*

My head felt so heavy I just couldn't explore any more tonight. As exhilarating as this introspection was, it was also exhausting. I'd have to tackle that last question about forgiving myself later.

For now I checked off the reasons in my head. The brutal honesty was gushing out of me now, and I was making some real progress.

1. I stayed because I believed marriage was forever, and I was compelled to honor that.
2. I stayed because I genuinely feared the wrath of Justin and I feared being alone.
3. I stayed because I believed in the good side of Justin.
4. I stayed because I couldn't handle acknowledging that I'd messed up one of the biggest decisions of my life.

———•———

The next week my friend Colleen came to visit from Ohio. We went out with a group of people from work, and one thing I noticed was how nice it was to be in the company of friends without the fear of a major blowup later.

Whenever Justin and I went out, I couldn't escape a sense of foreboding about what the alcohol would do to him, about what would happen once we got home with no one else around. It had been a long time since I'd enjoyed an evening out, and it was liberating.

Then Colleen asked about Justin.

This continued to be one of the most difficult repercussions for me—figuring out how to handle conversations about the divorce. While most people had been supportive, there had been some notable—and painful—exceptions. I shared with Colleen some of the reactions I'd been getting.

One of our colleagues had been saying some nasty things about me since news of the divorce got out. I shouldn't have been surprised since he was friends with Justin, and I could only imagine the version of events he'd heard. But I knew he wasn't alone.

Shortly after our separation was official, another friend and colleague warned me that word of the divorce was making the rounds about town. She told me she'd come to my defense when the public information officer she was interviewing for a story asked her about it. He, too, knew Justin fairly well.

"The PIO asked me if it was true that you'd had an affair—if that was why you left Justin. I told him, 'I know Christi, and I know she wouldn't do that. I think you should keep in mind that there are two sides to every story.' What was interesting was that then he said to me, 'Yeah, that's what I thought.' I could tell he didn't really believe what he'd heard."

She looked directly at me. "But I'm telling you straight up— I'm sure it came from Justin. I think you should confront him on it so he doesn't keep running his mouth."

I felt utterly torn. On the one hand, I was grateful to know someone was sticking up for me. Believed in me. Yet it really burned my cookie knowing my ex was running around spreading lies about me.

When lies are bleeding out, we want to do everything we can to get a tourniquet and halt the flow. But the fact is, we can't control what other people say about us.

We can, however, live a life that doesn't give their lies credence.

I knew confronting Justin wouldn't shut him up. It would probably just give him the satisfaction of knowing I was aware that his yapping was making the rounds at NASCAR speeds. One thing I'd learned by now was that nothing I could say would change how he chose to act.

Colleen helped me realize that this was one of those times I had to go into full-throttle faith mode.

"Can you change what Justin's going to say to people, Christi?" she asked.

"No," I admitted sheepishly.

"Then you just have to let it be and remember that in the end, the truth will always win."

I had to take comfort in the truth that ultimately Justin and I both knew what had happened. We both knew why I left. Whether anyone else ever fully understood wasn't the issue.

On top of that, my happiness couldn't hang on whether he ever truly understood, whether he took responsibility. That had to be his journey. I simply had to rest in the knowledge that I'd done all I could the best way I knew how.

Still, it's a tough pill to swallow—letting someone spout off blatantly false information about you through a megaphone. It can be downright paralyzing, and at times you feel desperate to defend yourself.

But for me, there was also a powerful lesson in it. These attacks on my reputation made me realize that the only people who know what really happens behind closed doors are the people behind them. All other commentary is just speculation.

I know I've been guilty of speculation in the past. I've found myself on the outside looking in, wondering, *What really happened? Did someone cheat? What drove them apart?* It's just human nature. And I'm a reporter, after all. If you don't have a healthy curiosity, then you're not doing your job.

But being on this side of things was an eye-opener. Having felt the rush of anxiety when people whispered behind my back, trying to dissect my relationship, I vowed not to be guilty of the same thing in the future. When I'm tempted to judge others, I try to remind myself what it's like to be on the other side of that fence—the fence that separates the players from the spectators. As I've learned firsthand, watching the game isn't the same as playing it. So when I'm on the sidelines and I feel judgment creeping in, I ask God to forgive me and to give me a more gracious, humble heart.

If it matters to us, it matters to Him. And if it hurts us, it hurts Him.

It was shortly after my visit with Colleen that one of my mantras was born. Back in my town house one particularly difficult day as I was trying to sort through the chaos of the last six months, I said this prayer: "God, I invite You into this moment, and I give all this to You." It was short and sweet, but it was enough to help me step back. It gave me a second to breathe and think about what I needed to do next. It opened my mind to a new way of thinking—a hopeful view rather than a pessimistic one.

The funny thing is that when you truly let go and surrender what you're dealing with to God, He takes all of those things.

That's exactly what He has been waiting for—for us to trust Him enough to give it all to Him. He's never too busy to deal with our problems. He's not too angry with us for being less than perfect. He's not too ashamed of us for thinking our love life or our finances or our grief needs His attention. Our issues aren't too small for Him—He's just as tuned in to us as He is to the devastation in Sudan and the wars in the Middle East. If it matters to us, it matters to Him. And if it hurts us, it hurts Him. He's ready to help us change . . . if we're ready to ask Him.

And I was finally ready. Once I got that and began the process of surrender, I no longer felt helpless. I was on the path to becoming what I craved—fearless.

Years later, after I moved to Atlanta, I heard a one-liner I wish I would have come across when I was going through this whole fiasco. My pastor Vic Pentz said, "You know the only difference between us and God? God doesn't think He's us."

Vic was right. Who among us hasn't tried to play God with our lives, deluding ourselves into thinking we could understand it all and control it all? And how often have we found ourselves in a pit after trying to drive that truckload of chaos on our own?

But we never run out of chances with God. We may make mistakes again and again, but He holds out His hand every time, happy to pick us up out of the mayhem we've made.

We never run out of chances with God.

God uses imperfect people, and I fit that bill perfectly. He counters my incompetence, my weakness, my arrogance. And He responds with forgiveness.

I remembered a passage I'd read by Beth Moore: "Our self-condemning hearts can't block our forgiveness, but they can keep us from feeling forgiven. The result will be a twisted resignation to our own capacity to sin rather than any confidence in God's capacity to restore us."

I shuddered to think how many times in the past several years I'd made the mistake of confusing faith in myself with faith in God. I'd let myself down so much I couldn't even identify who I was anymore. Now, sitting alone in my home, with only Bruno asleep at my side, I had a renewed sense of who I was.

I was a child of God.

As imperfect and fractured as we are at times, we give up on ourselves long before God ever will. Yes, we will tumble. But He's ready to open the gates of grace every time we fall.

There is strength in surrender . . . as long as we're surrendering to Him.

CHAPTER 15

YOUR WORTH IS INTACT, RIGHT NOW

JUSTIN AND I finally came to some financial agreements regarding the divorce, but he refused to sign the settlement. It included harassment stipulations, and he wasn't about to sign his name to that.

After I'd told my legal adviser about some of the late-night phone calls and combative, belligerent messages Justin had been leaving me, he believed it was important to stipulate that any harassment would cost Justin—not necessarily monetarily, but in some capacity. So we were yet again hashing out the verbiage of the contract.

Even so, the divorce wasn't consuming me like it used to. I actually felt somewhat disconnected from the situation at that point, as though it were just a technicality. Which, in many ways, was accurate. But I couldn't ignore the reality that while the past might not be holding me hostage, it certainly hadn't abandoned its grip on me.

One day when a girlfriend and I were talking about fashion sense, she casually said, "Oh, you've got great taste in shoes! You're such a shoe whore." I knew she meant nothing by it, but that word *whore* just crawled up my spine. I couldn't believe how deeply Justin's comments were seared into the core of my being.

I talked to a friend of mine about how I wasn't letting go of things the way I wanted to. She referred me to a doctor she knew in Chicago named Dr. Amelia Case, who guides people through a series of questions that help move you toward a life of gratitude and certainty about the truth and about yourself. These questions help you neutralize antagonistic thoughts so they no longer control you.

I had to admit I'd never heard of such therapy, so I called Dr. Case myself. Fortunately these were sessions I could do over the phone, which was convenient since we lived a couple of thousand miles apart.

"We all have perceptions of our past, whether from relationships or events, and those perceptions can be polarizing," she told me. "These perceptions rule our present lives. In other words, we're still allowing feelings from the past to dictate our current state of mind."

Okay. This much I understood. This had been my reality for some time.

So we started to tackle that concept—that something as simple as a word or two could send my view of myself into a tailspin. I didn't buy it completely at first. Just one word had that kind of power over me? No way. But as we talked more, I began to absorb what a devastating effect verbal abuse can have—and how long-lasting it can be. It sits in a dark corner, just waiting to sneak up on us and pounce on our insecurities.

Dr. Case started by inquiring about my relationship with Justin. We talked about the divorce and my desire to discard any harsh feelings I had about him and about myself. I told her that my goal was to toss out all my baggage so I could fly freely—so I could live a life of authenticity.

Dr. Case then began asking me specific questions about the past four years. How would I describe my relationship with Justin then? Now? What things did he say to me that frightened me? In what ways did he make me feel worthless? The questions forced me to look squarely at the verbal abuse itself—the specific words Justin used to berate me. I didn't want to relive it, but suddenly I knew that was exactly what I had to do in order to amputate it from my life.

As I relayed to Dr. Case the names he called me and the threats he hurled at me, she replied, "Ah, now we're getting somewhere. Okay, the first question for you: how are you a whore?"

Bam! I felt a ten-ton weight crashing down on me. What did she just say? Did she call me a whore?

I started coaching myself silently. *No, Christi. Listen to the question. How are you a whore?*

I sat there for a minute, and for the life of me, I couldn't make heads or tails of the question. It was so offensive! I didn't even want to address it. But I had faith that Dr. Case knew what she was doing, so I tried to strong-arm myself into honestly answering. Here's the thing—I was utterly baffled. After a few more seconds of silence, Dr. Case stepped in.

"Let's think about this," she said. "How are you a whore in your job?"

Uh . . . okay. More silence. I still had no idea what she expected me to say. So she took the wheel again.

"Let me help you out: (a) you sell yourself; (b) you have to look great to do it; (c) you work to make others choose you over other women in a lineup; (d) you're aware that the more people choose you, the more you get paid. How's that for a start?"

I was dumbfounded! She'd just compared my job as a journalist to being a whore . . . and it actually made some sense. She was taking the very weapons Justin had used against me and giving me the power to take some of the poison out of them.

Initially I fought the comparison. Even as I felt my brain bending toward understanding, toward neutralizing that word, I found myself resisting. I didn't want to admit that my job was anything like being a whore. But I was gradually gaining a new perspective from which to view that one simple word—a word that up until now had made my skin crawl like no other.

Dr. Case left me with a homework assignment: I was to continue thinking about her last question and add answers to those she had already given me. By the time we hung up, my head was aching. It was as though the strenuous mental exercise of trying to reposition my thoughts had caused physical pain to my body.

I spent a couple of days ruminating on this assignment. As I did, I felt the punch of the dreaded word slowly fading. When I heard the word *whore* in my mind, it didn't have the same sting to it. Now, don't get me wrong—it still wasn't a word I'd use to describe anyone, but the edge it once had in regard to me was softening.

As I was considering all this, a lightbulb went off in my head. I was amazed at the gravity of words—how a simple utterance can act as a chain, binding us to a perception for much of our lives. When words are used against us—intentionally or not—we often become imprisoned by them. If we can start seeing those words from a new angle, we are freed from their power. And in my case, I was also freed from the man who targeted me with those words.

———•———

I was making some progress with my own perceptions, but the anxiety about how other people might see the divorce wasn't dissipating. That was the next concept Dr. Case worked with me on: seeing myself as God sees me and loving myself despite what anyone else might think.

The sooner we realize that God doesn't judge us the way the world does—or maybe even worse, the way *we* judge ourselves—the sooner we're going to realize that we have worth. Imperfect parts and all.

Here's where true transformation begins: when we realize how valuable we are in God's eyes. Then we'll be able to accept ourselves as human beings, and we'll be able to accept everyone else as humans too. Not as larger-than-life perfect people who have it all together all the time.

Take it from a reformed Anxious Annie like me. Spend too much time sizing yourself up against everyone else, and you're bound to tumble into a trench so deep you won't be able to recognize another human when that person is standing two inches away.

All of us have secret insecurities we're dealing with, hidden struggles we try to conceal. Whether we realize it or not, we're all in this together. We're fighting the same inner battle. We need to tune out the lies the world feeds us—that if we don't have the looks or the money or the man, then we're not worth the effort. The truth is, our worth and dignity are fully intact. Right here. Right now. God designed you specifically to be *you*, and no one can take that away. When you know your sense of worth is from Him, you don't need to rely on someone else to give it to you. And *that* is freedom.

There was a fresh stream of hope springing up in this parched land. I wanted to stand in its flow and get drenched. Covered in hope from head to toe.

As I was driving home from work one afternoon, I was overcome by the enormity of that freedom. The mountains surrounding Phoenix were stunning to me, as always. But on that day, they were stunning in a new way. I used to look at those mountains and feel like a prisoner. When I was married to Justin, those bluffs were like a jail cell that kept me imprisoned in this parched valley. Now they looked majestic and adventurous—as though they were inviting me to explore them and see what joys lay beyond their borders.

I found it intriguing that the exact same scenery could exude two completely different emotions based on my perspective. I wasn't afraid or resentful of those mountains anymore. There was a fresh stream of hope springing up in this parched land. I wanted to stand in its flow and get drenched. Covered in hope from head to toe.

———•———

Still, my emotions were like those mountains—one minute as high as the peaks and just hours later as low as the trenches between them. That night I had another appointment on the phone with Dr. Case, and this time we really got down to the nuts and bolts. I had to address those feelings of unworthiness that lingered in my head. I felt like such a mess!

"God didn't create a mess, Christi," she told me. "On the whole or in parts. He has made you just right the way you are. Your greatest challenge is to thank God for the way He has made you—every minute, not just during what you perceive as your 'best minutes.' Do you think you—or any thoughts you have—escape God's ever-present view?"

Wow, I thought. *And He loves me anyway?* This was big.

My homework was a series of questions Dr. Case formed out of our conversation. One question was particularly daunting: "What would have been the drawback if Justin had been a sweet angel and had never been mean to you or scared you?"

Seriously? There would have been a drawback to being treated like a valued human being?

Ouch. Yeah, I guess I was still harboring some resentment there.

I took some time to let this all sink in. If Justin had been wonderful and kind to me, what would have been the detriment in that?

I started thinking about where I was at that moment.

Slowly, a thought from an entirely different corner of my mind started taking shape in my head.

If Justin had been a wonderful husband, I thought, *I'd still be with him.* I would have missed out on the life, the freedom, the faith I've come to appreciate so much. I would have missed out on this journey back to who I was meant to be. I would have missed out on the exhilaration of living a life of authenticity and peace.

Dr. Case asked me to find ten answers to that seemingly impossible query. As soon as we hung up, I started typing ferociously as thought after thought, revelation after revelation, popped into my head.

What would have been the drawback if Justin had been a sweet angel and had never been mean to me or scared me?

1. I wouldn't have learned to lean on God so much.
2. I wouldn't know how strong I am.
3. I wouldn't have learned about taking risks.
4. My faith wouldn't have expanded so much.
5. I wouldn't have had the opportunity to be introspective and examine who I really am.
6. I wouldn't have learned that I'm capable of forgiving someone who hurt me badly.
7. I wouldn't have learned that I can forgive myself for my shortcomings.
8. I wouldn't have learned that I can forgive someone and still extract him or her from my life.
9. I wouldn't have learned that forgiveness doesn't mean condoning what someone did.
10. I wouldn't have learned to recognize potentially harmful behavior in the future.
11. I wouldn't be able to help other people who have experienced similar situations.

12. I wouldn't have learned that forgiveness doesn't equate to weakness; it's one of the strongest, bravest decisions a person can make.

13. I wouldn't have learned that I'd rather be alone than be with the wrong person.

14. I wouldn't have realized that money or a nice home doesn't bring true security.

15. I wouldn't have realized that simply being married isn't a guarantee against loneliness.

16. I wouldn't have opened my heart to change.

17. I wouldn't have learned how detrimental it can be to judge people.

18. I wouldn't have learned the power of words.

19. I wouldn't have learned the power of friendships.

20. I wouldn't have learned that it's okay to lean on friends so much.

21. I wouldn't have learned to choose my words wisely.

22. I wouldn't have learned true humility.

23. I wouldn't have learned to hold on for dear life to hope.

24. I wouldn't have discovered that what doesn't kill you makes you stronger.

25. I wouldn't have discovered the importance of authenticity.

26. I wouldn't have discovered that being married doesn't guarantee happiness.

27. I wouldn't have realized that no matter how far we stray from God's plan for us, if we finally surrender to Him, He'll lead us back to the correct path.

28. I wouldn't know the thrill of second chances.

The list was pouring out of me. One reason after another to be grateful that Justin had *not* been a loving, supportive husband. It was crazy—but exhilarating!

When I sent the list to Dr. Case, I got a response that stirred me. "I honestly have a tear of inspiration in my eye after reading this again," she wrote. "There is a lot of wisdom here. It sounds like you have been given a gift of freedom combined with a new appreciation for what you have."

Then Dr. Case pushed me even further.

"If you could say something to Justin now, would it be 'Thank you' rather than 'I forgive you'?"

I thought about that for a second. "I'd have to say I would tell Justin I'm grateful for the time we had together because it taught me so much. There is a part of me, however, that would want to hold back the 'thank you' because I never saw him take responsibility for his actions in our relationship." I remembered how he would deflect any blame of his own and shoot it back at me. "If I thanked him, I think it would only add to his narcissism," I said. "He'd twist it into taking credit for helping me."

I didn't want Justin to suffer. I truly wanted him to be happy. But from my human perspective, I also wanted him to own up to his own actions and accept how they contributed to the breakup.

I took a deep breath. What a breakthrough! This kind of mental work was, indeed, fatiguing, but it was also pivotal to healing. It was the only way to be freed from the teeth of the animal that was still gnawing away inside.

CHAPTER 16

GOD HAS NO LIMITS

I COULD SENSE that not only was my mind opening but my heart was too. Bit by bit, I was allowing myself to believe. To accept that I could live differently. The shackles from the verbal assaults were finally starting to loosen their grip.

Believing that things can change is one of the most daunting choices we'll ever have to make. But this hope is necessary, because it's the first step toward putting change in motion. Whether it's our circumstances or our perspective, a transformation *will* take shape.

I thought back to a couple of weeks before, when I was driving home after a difficult confrontation with Justin. He'd called to give me grief about a couple of things we still couldn't agree on in the divorce. As I was processing all the hurtful things he'd said to me and trying to muster the strength to make it through, I stopped at a traffic light and let out a big sigh. Then I looked up, and through teary eyes, I saw a bumper sticker on the car in front of me. It said, "God has no limits." It was a tangible reminder to me that things *could* change—because no matter how big my problems were, God was even bigger.

A couple of weeks later, as I crawled into bed, I opened my devotions for some last inspiring words for the day. What I read was a beautiful reminder of how little I have control of and how vast and promising God is, even when I have no idea what's coming.

Then I came to a line that might as well have been written precisely for me. The words by A. J. Russell read, "Just go step by step. My will shall be revealed as you go. . . . Never limit my power. It is limitless."

My eyes were as big as saucers. I'd walked through my whole thirty-one years of life, never once having heard that phrase. And here it was for the second time in two weeks, blaring right at me. Obviously God was trying to tell me something, and that something, I think, was, "Relax. And believe." I needed to let God do His thing in my life without trying to control it on my own.

"God, help my unbelief," I whispered. "And thank You for not confining me to the limits I put on myself."

I needed to hang on to that message, because the next night wasn't so peaceful. Once again I was fielding phone calls from Justin, who was saying heinous things about me and my whole family, cursing the entire time. He was making fun of where I came from—my sweet, little town—saying it was going to die out and become nothing, just like me.

He accused me of sleeping around, of not being good at my job, of being a joke to people in town. I felt my neck getting warm with anger, and my shoulders started shaking with that old fear. He went on to say that a couple of his friends had told him he was better off without me. They said they couldn't understand why we'd gotten together in the first place because, basically, I wasn't in his league.

I finally told him he was being pathetic and hung up on him—twice. But I couldn't disconnect from the anger that was raging in me now. How could I ever have been with a man who said such spiteful things? Who seemed to take such pleasure in attacking me?

It was baffling to me that someone I'd once been so in love with was now someone I couldn't wait to get away from. How does that happen? How can one person provoke such diametrically opposed emotions? How do we end up making such inexplicable choices about who to let into our lives?

I don't know the answer to that, but I do know that although we can't change what happened, we can certainly learn to recognize the good that came out of those decisions. And somewhere, in some way, there's a valuable lesson in every whacked-out situation we experience. If we're willing to dig deep to find it.

In an attempt to resolve my anger, I turned to my new assignment from Dr. Case: "Find one hundred benefits to Justin's verbally abusive, intimidating, power-seeking behavior."

Who was she kidding? One hundred? I'd be lucky to find one! I continued reading.

"Yes, one hundred." Obviously this woman could read my mind. She knew when I saw that number, I'd assume she was off her rocker. "Specifically, how did his persona benefit you and help you define your highest values?"

She gave a word of warning: "Caution: a benefit isn't 'avoiding him' or 'knowing I'd never be like that.' Put the benefits in words of real value that don't support your current perception that he's bad."

Ugh! In the famous phrase of *Seinfeld*'s Elaine, "Get out!"

This seemed utterly impossible.

I sat there with my head in my hands. How could verbal abuse possibly be beneficial to me—or to anyone?

I urged my mind to view this from another angle. It's hard to make a mental shift when you've been approaching things from a place of pain for so long. But this is the hard truth: we can't erase what happened to us. Whatever giant we're battling, whatever it is we're fleeing, whatever injustice we're trying to get over, it happened. We can't change that. But we can change what we take away from it. We can change how we let it affect us. It doesn't have to rule our lives. But we're the only ones who can cut that rope to free ourselves.

We can't erase what happened to us. Whatever giant we're battling, whatever it is we're fleeing, whatever injustice we're trying to get over, it happened. We can't change that. But we can change what we take away from it.

I allowed my mind to go back to some of those humiliating moments with Justin—the verbal beatings, the words I couldn't bring myself to repeat, and the immense shame I felt—not just in the moment of verbal impact but afterward.

Then I moved my thoughts from those moments to the one I was in now: a peaceful place where I didn't live in fear.

Suddenly I recognized that the hideous words helped drive me to where I currently was. Here I was, alone, and to my surprise, that was good.

I sat in front of the computer and wrote, "Benefits of Verbal Abuse."

Even writing it felt sick on some level. But I forced myself to view this from a new angle. The typing started slowly this time, interspersed with moments of silence. But gradually the thoughts started flowing more steadily until they were downright spirited.

Benefits of Verbal Abuse

1. Brought me closer to God
2. Helped me really appreciate my family
3. Helped me redefine what security means
4. Helped me recognize my need for a role model
5. Helped me pray more
6. Helped me learn boundaries
7. Helped me realize the importance of words
8. Encouraged me to confide in my friends
9. Shaped my view of myself as an individual who is meant for more than abuse
10. Helped me realize that I was not serving God in my relationship and that I wanted to seek ways to serve Him
11. Helped me be more empathetic to people in similar situations
12. Encouraged me to reach out to people in similar situations
13. Ultimately softened my heart
14. Helped me appreciate my friends more

15. Encouraged me to be introspective about myself and my motives

16. Expanded my capacity to forgive others

17. Expanded my capacity to forgive myself

18. Released me from being so critical of my shortcomings

19. Helped me learn I'm not a bad person

20. Solidified my belief that second chances do exist

21. Helped me overcome my fear of being alone

22. Encouraged my independence

23. Taught me humility

24. Taught me to love myself

25. Taught me the value of communication—both words and actions

26. Helped me realize the importance of selflessness

27. Taught me that others are kind and willing to help

28. Taught me to fight for what I know is right

29. Helped me realize other people aren't blind to people's pain

30. Taught me that the most important things in life aren't things

31. Taught me that money is not security

32. Taught me that I'm not my mistakes

33. Showed me that my mistakes don't define all that I am

34. Showed me I'm worth something to others

35. Prompted me to work harder at my career

36. Prompted me to care more about my health

37. Prompted me to take better care of myself emotionally and spiritually

38. Helped me reach out to others for help

39. Helped me appreciate silence
40. Helped me make wise decisions about who to let into my life
41. Helped me take notice of people who don't have my best interests at heart
42. Helped me appreciate and seek authentic relationships
43. Helped me realize I am responsible for only myself
44. Helped me realize I can't control anyone else or any situation
45. Helped me take a deep look at who I want to be
46. Helped me trust God
47. Gave me strength to walk away from harmful situations I can't control
48. Taught me that I'm compassionate
49. Taught me that it's possible to heal from any circumstance if it's handed over to God
50. Taught me to fend for myself
51. Helped me realize what I will and will not allow in my life
52. Taught me that I'm more intelligent than I give myself credit for
53. Taught me I'm stronger than I thought I was
54. Taught me to listen more
55. Taught me that I'd rather be alone than be with the wrong person
56. Taught me to value myself
57. Taught me to value my relationships
58. Taught me who I *don't* want to be
59. Taught me to realize that nothing is ever hopeless

60. Taught me to take responsibility for my actions and words
61. Taught me to be calm in the midst of harrowing situations
62. Helped me to never give up on others
63. Helped me face my fears

Well, it wasn't one hundred, but it was a good start.

I perused my list again and saw a few themes.

First of all, there was a new independence in me. I was becoming a strong woman who was overcoming my fears and wasn't afraid to take chances. Because let's face it—leaving a marriage is taking a chance. But I knew in my case it was a chance worth taking.

Second, there was a theme of gratitude in this list. Gratitude for the people I knew, the things I'd learned, the boundaries I'd identified. I was a little surprised to find I was now exuding gratefulness.

The third theme I saw was forgiveness. As I searched my list, I realized there weren't any bitter words or biting accusations. I didn't write, "I learned never to allow an idiot into my life again." Forgiveness didn't mean denying what had happened. It didn't mean rewinding the past and blacking out the hurtful words that had been said. It didn't mean pretending there was no longer any pain. But it did mean I could use this experience to grow. To find guidance. To be strengthened. To heal.

One night as I lay in bed reading, I was again wrestling with guilt for leaving Justin. I struggled with feeling so fulfilled and free while he was obviously hurting.

I opened my book to read, and I immediately came across a line that pierced my soul: "The fact that we forgive someone does not mean that we can never leave that person." The book went on to talk about the difference between a safe partner and a dangerous partner. If someone truly loves you, he doesn't knowingly put his foot in your way to trip you, and he doesn't criticize you for being a klutz when you fall. Instead, he can see when you're trying and won't punish you if you fail.

I felt like the author was looking straight at me! As I read the passage again, I had no question which category my relationship with Justin fell into. He was a dangerous partner for me.

My mind faded back to a Sunday afternoon a few years before. I was sick and needed to go to a clinic, but Justin wanted to stay home and watch football. As I walked out the door, he called after me to let him know if I needed anything.

We'd just moved to Phoenix. I didn't know a soul.

The clinic's doctor thought I'd suffered some sort of poisoning from paint fumes, and he sent me to the emergency room at a local hospital. In the packed waiting room, I called Justin to tell him where I was. He simply said, "Okay, well, call me if you need anything." I just stood there staring at the phone.

Then I called my father because I needed to hear a comforting voice. I played it down, telling him this was no big deal—that I just wanted to tell him what was going on.

I hung up, walked over to a chair in the waiting room, and sat down. As I sat there, surrounded by a bunch of people I didn't know, in an unfamiliar city, waiting to see a doctor I'd never met, the isolation and emptiness started to overcome me. And worst of all, my husband was nowhere to be found.

I was surrounded by people, but I was alone.

I felt worthless.

A short time later, Justin walked in and marched over to me. "How are you feeling?" He was clearly annoyed.

"About the same. I'm glad you're here."

He plopped down in a seat next to me and looked right in my eyes. "You didn't have to call your dad!" he hissed.

Oh. Now I got it. He came because my dad called him.

An hour later, after X rays and examinations, the doctor told me I had pleurisy.

"It's an infection in the lining of your lungs that makes it feel like knives are piercing your chest and back with every breath," he said. "It's a virus, so I can only give you medication to try to alleviate the pain. I'm afraid you also have pneumonia. I think we might need to admit you to the hospital overnight."

I watched Justin's face morph from agitation to confusion. His demeanor changed completely, as he sat up from his slumped position and his ears perked up. Suddenly I realized that he hadn't believed me until now! He thought I'd been lying or embellishing things. And I wondered, *How much weight do my words hold with him? Does he believe me? And does he even care?*

As I thought about Justin in terms of safe or not safe, another moment from our marriage popped into my head. I'd been working at KTVK for a mere six months when I did a consumer piece about furniture—comparing prices between two stores that sold the same product. The store that had been inflating their prices pulled their advertising after the report, and I had to give a deposition to our station attorney the next day. I was sweating bullets! Now, the store wasn't claiming my story was wrong, just that it was damaging to them. I knew I'd done my job and had done it well, but it was still nerve racking.

When I confided to Justin about my raw nerves, I thought he'd understand—maybe even give me a little reassurance. But here's what I got: "For Christ's sake, if you can't handle this business, then just quit! If you can't hack it, you should get out and find something else to do!" I sat on the couch, stunned. So much for moral support.

Once again that feeling of worthlessness soaked into my bones.

The store never resumed advertising with our station, but my bosses and the general manager stood behind me. Phil said, "You did everything right, Christi. They're just ticked off because you called them on the carpet."

Funny, my boss had my back, but my husband didn't.

A safe partner builds you up. A dangerous one tears you down. I knew full well what the latter felt like: fear.

Fear lived with me for four years. It sat dormant for a while, yes, but it followed me, like my shadow, just waiting for the next bout of drunkenness or fit of rage to swoop in and terrify me. I suppose I shouldn't have been surprised that fear didn't automatically go away just because Justin did. But I knew I needed to work on releasing it so I could live the authentic life I craved. We owe it to ourselves to loosen the grip of that fear. Love doesn't have to hurt. It shouldn't. Not like it did with Justin.

Every time he drank, that angst would kick in for me. I think once someone lays a hand on you or even threatens to do so, the fear that he'll do it again never vanishes. Especially when the origin of the anger—his drinking, in our case—is still present. When you don't take the cause out of the equation, you can't take the fear out of it either.

Love doesn't guarantee that your feelings will never be bruised or that you'll never be angry or upset. But love should offer both people a safe place. Physical, verbal, or emotional abuse is not love. Period.

God didn't put us on this earth to live with someone who steals our joy and our security, whether that's through words or violence. That isn't our destiny.

———•———

A couple of days and several nasty phone calls later, I was about at my wit's end. Justin had been calling at night with his usual threats about how he had deep pockets and he'd make me pay for this divorce. I usually just hung up on him, but that morning I heard a different Justin over the phone.

"I'm sorry about the other night, Christi. I don't want to do this anymore. I'm done. I'm signing the papers today." He sounded resolute but also a bit defeated. And exhausted.

God didn't put us on this earth to live with someone who steals our joy and our security, whether that's through words or violence. That isn't our destiny.

"Thank you," I said. It was all I could get out. I hated to hear him hurting, but I was relieved to know it was finally going to be over.

The following week I sat in my attorney's office. I didn't hesitate as he handed me one paper after another for my signature.

I signed my name. My given name. Christi Paul. I knew I'd never have to sign Christi Barnes again, and it felt good. We shook hands, and I left his office almost skipping. I had no regrets, no sadness. Only a twinge of remorse that things had to come to this.

I found myself hesitating as I put the key in the ignition. Sitting in my car in that parking lot, I took a moment to think. My mind flashed back to the scene six months earlier, when I was sitting in another parking lot—the church parking lot after the gigantic blowup with Justin. Back then, a moment like this had felt impossible. I remembered the heaviness of that day—the moment I realized I had to leave but had no clue how to facilitate it, let alone find the strength to do it.

Now I stared at the orange trees and the beams of sunlight streaming through the leaves as they swayed in the brisk winter air. The stillness seemed to envelop me as I breathed deeply. I thought of Justin and how he'd feel when he got the call that I'd signed the papers. That it was officially over. A pang of sadness swooped in—but just for a moment.

"God," I prayed, "please be with Justin. Help him find his own peace, his own joy, his own way. Forgive me for the pain I've caused and for not listening to You sooner. But thank You for not making me pay for that for the rest of my life. Thank You for giving me strength and wisdom. Thank You for showering me with your grace. Please do the same for Justin."

Then the realization kicked in that I was free. Really, truly free—in every sense of the word. Until it was official, I don't think it was possible for me to believe it. That day it was real.

Since Justin signed the papers first, I kind of felt as though he were giving me permission to go my way. Not that I needed it, and not that I was foolish enough to think I had his blessing, but it was official.

Hello, world! I'm Christi Paul, and I've missed you! Now let's get this life restarted.

CHAPTER 17

YOU CAN BE GRATEFUL AND STILL WANT MORE

BEFORE I MOVED into my own space, my soul had been almost as parched as the Phoenix desert. But as I got settled on my own, the cool, cleansing water of authenticity started pouring in.

With each new day I was discovering another liberty I'd forgotten I had. The freedom to walk through my day on a solid foundation, without dodging land mines of verbal barrages. The freedom to laugh as loud as my heart desired without a disapproving glare being shot my way. The freedom to get whatever I wanted at a restaurant without anyone making me feel stupid for ordering it.

As I walked through my new reality, I realized it wasn't just the gigantic blowups behind closed doors that had made things difficult. It was also the less obvious moments of tension that piled up day after day.

As I sat outside a restaurant sipping hot chocolate, a memory about an incident that happened several years before suddenly hit me.

The outside heat had been almost unbearable, but the cold blasts of air inside the restaurant made me cold. So I ordered hot chocolate . . . only to be met by a huffing grunt from my then-husband. He shook his head, and right in front of the server, he said, "What are you doing?"

I felt like a complete idiot.

"It's 105 degrees outside, and you want hot chocolate?" he hurled.

I could feel myself shriveling into the chair. The server, obviously uncomfortable, said, "I can see if we can make some for you," before hurrying away as quickly as possible.

I felt so ashamed back then. I wore that coat of humiliation so many times I wore it out.

Sitting in that booth now, I recognized what a different person I was because of all that had happened. I was a cocktail of sorts: my hopeful pre-Justin self, mixed with a cautious post-Justin persona, with a splash of spanking-new vibrancy added in. I had faith that God would bring out a newer, wiser version of myself on the other side. I still had my insecurities and imperfections, thank you, but I was learning to embrace them and grow from them. And I was clinging to hope about whatever was ahead.

I was still, however, trying to learn gratitude for all that happened before.

If I could say something to Justin now, would it be "Thank you" rather than "I forgive you"?

The question from Dr. Case echoed in my ears.

I want to, God, I prayed silently. *I want to be able to appreciate that time with Justin enough to be able to thank him for it. But I just can't feel it yet.*

———•———

In a recent conversation with Dr. Case, we zeroed in on something about me: I'd been habituating the belief that I was allowed to have only so much happiness.

For example, if my professional life was going well, then I figured my personal life wouldn't be so hot, or vice versa. Or worse yet, I didn't deserve the happiness I had, so surely it would be taken away soon enough.

This is what Dr. Case wrote in a follow-up e-mail. Simple and direct, yet profound. "You can be grateful and still want more. It doesn't negate your gratitude."

Immediately I balked at her words. How could I want for more? Wouldn't God think I was ungrateful? Wouldn't He think, *What, haven't I given you enough already?* I knew there were a lot of people who needed a lot more than I did. I had food. I had shelter. I had clothes. Wouldn't God think I was acting like a spoiled brat for wanting more?

He yearns to give us so much more than what we're asking for—if only we'd believe it's possible. If only we'd believe He loves us that much, that graciously.

My automatic push back set off an alarm in my head. Maybe this was another place where I didn't "get" God.

Just like that moment in the church parking lot when I finally saw the image of God as Father, not some omnipotent being lurking above, waiting for us to screw up so He can hail down punishment on us. Rather, He's a father who wants to embrace us. Help us. Carry us, if need be. He yearns to give us so much more than what we're asking for—if only we'd believe it's possible. If only we'd believe He loves us that much, that graciously.

The thing about grace is that by very definition, it can't be earned. It's a gift. We don't have to be perfect to receive it, but we do have to be willing. Willing to open our minds and our hearts. Willing to believe.

Grace isn't just raining down on everyone else, my friend. You're in that rainstorm too.

I'd always been perplexed by this verse from the book of Matthew:

Keep on asking, and you will receive what you ask for.
Keep on seeking, and you will find. Keep on knocking,
and the door will be opened to you.

MATTHEW 7:7 (NLT)

This promise perturbs a lot of us because we've asked for so many things that didn't happen. We've made ourselves vulnerable, and then we feel like God has turned His back on us. "Hey, You said we could ask! What gives?"

Grace isn't just raining down on everyone else. You're in that rainstorm too.

I had asked God for answers about Melissa's death. I'd asked Him to save P.A. I'd asked Him to save my marriage, for heaven's sake! How could I trust this verse?

Even as I asked the question, this is what popped into my mind: *You don't just trust a verse, Christi. You trust God.*

There's only one way to get good at believing, and that's like anything else: you practice it. On more than one occasion I'd begged God to help my unbelief. I wasn't sure at the time if I thought He'd really do it. It's kind of a crazy concept, isn't it? We pray for help to believe, but we don't believe we'll get it. We're afraid to believe God will do what we ask, because what if it doesn't come true? And what if the disappointment crushes us?

We forget to be grateful for what we have, because we're so focused on the fact that we haven't gotten what we've been praying for.

Here's what I've learned along the way, though: don't be afraid to believe. Don't make the mistake of thinking you can earn God's blessings. You can't. Grace is already pouring down on you. In buckets.

But so many of us are holding umbrellas over our heads, trying to protect ourselves from what we fear, that we can't recognize the abundance God is showering on us. We're fighting it ourselves, and we don't even know it.

The other problem we have is that if that thing we're asking for doesn't happen soon enough, we get frustrated. We pull away. We forget to be grateful for what we have, because we're so focused on the fact that we haven't gotten what we've been praying for. Gratitude really does change the way we see.

And you know what I was really grateful for right at that moment as I sat outside on my patio watching Bruno explore and dig in the dirt? It was a thought that reverberated through every muscle in my body: God gives us second chances to get it right.

As I reflected on the last year, I couldn't deny how God seemed to start giving me more and more to be grateful for as I let loose that thankfulness. It's like when you can't wait to give a gift to someone—a gift you've spent significant time and effort choosing to make sure it's exactly what they'll love. You can't wait to see their reaction, right? I think God is like that. The more our gratefulness exudes from us, the more He wants to give us . . . because He knows the gifts will be received with a grateful heart.

———•———

My gratefulness was often diluted, though, with guilt—the guilt of hurting Justin. I'd done so much honest work to try to plunge those feelings into oblivion, but I couldn't seem to escape them.

I knew I didn't want to live in avoidance again. I wanted to face my demons head-on. So one night I addressed this in a conversation with Dr. Case.

"This struggle with my guilt seems so debilitating sometimes!" I confessed. "And it won't let go!"

She talked with me for a while, then left me with some homework, including this question: "What would be the drawback if you never had any kind of struggle?"

Hmm . . . no struggles at all? So with the snap of my fingers I'd win the lotto, lose those extra ten pounds that seem glued to my thighs, and gain the wisdom of age without the wrinkles that go with them? What's the drawback in that?

But seriously, enough of the superficiality. I'll play.

After we hung up, I quieted my mind and sat down to explore the question. And so my next list was born.

Over a forty-minute period, here's what I wrote:

The Drawback of Never Having Struggles

    1. I wouldn't turn to God as much.

    2. I wouldn't consider other people as much.

3. I wouldn't appreciate what I have.

4. I wouldn't learn to do better—to see things differently.

5. I wouldn't push myself to do more.

6. I wouldn't relate to other people's struggles as well.

7. I wouldn't appreciate other people's kindness as much.

8. I wouldn't be as humble.

9. I wouldn't have as much empathy for other people.

10. I wouldn't learn to toughen up.

11. I wouldn't learn the importance of having courage.

12. I wouldn't realize how important faith is.

13. I might buy the lie that life should be smooth sailing.

14. I wouldn't learn to rely on other people who want to help me.

15. I wouldn't be able to help other people with similar struggles.

16. I wouldn't form such close bonds with people.

17. I wouldn't learn patience.

18. I wouldn't learn to trust a God I can't see.

19. I wouldn't realize that I can't control everything.

20. I wouldn't learn from my mistakes.

21. I wouldn't learn to identify my own contributions to the struggle.

22. I wouldn't learn to get up after I fall.

23. I wouldn't learn to anticipate the unexpected.

24. I wouldn't learn to take risks.

25. I wouldn't learn to persevere.

26. I wouldn't learn that one struggle or imperfection isn't the end.

27. I wouldn't learn authenticity.

28. I wouldn't know the sense of accomplishment from working through a struggle.

29. I wouldn't know the feeling of relief after a struggle.

30. I wouldn't build my character.

31. I wouldn't learn to prioritize what's important.

32. I wouldn't know how to laugh through some of the tough times, acknowledging that a struggle isn't the end of the world.

33. I wouldn't learn how to avoid other struggles in the future.

34. I wouldn't know the value of teamwork in facing a struggle.

35. I'd miss witnessing the kindness and compassion of people who come to my aid.

36. I wouldn't learn to recognize what I can and can't control.

37. I wouldn't learn about surrendering what I can't control.

38. I wouldn't learn how to fight for what I can control.

I looked back over my list. *So struggles actually serve us?* That sounded impossible until I got things down on paper.

It's only when we start to view our struggles from an entirely different lens—when we identify the benefits in them—that we can finally let go of them.

We don't have to let struggles steamroll us. We don't have to fear them. In fact, we can be grateful for them because they can make us more intrepid and resilient . . . if we let them.

CHAPTER 18

GUARD YOUR THOUGHTS; WHAT YOU THINK, YOU BECOME

As THE WEEKS ticked by, I was frustrated to find that Justin's criticisms were still alive and churning in my head. The name-calling and accusations, the inadequacy, the feelings of incompetency. They were all still there on some level. I never wanted to hand him that power, and I knew he couldn't have it . . . unless I gave it to him. But it felt impossible to unleash those memories. If I was going to move on, Justin's words would have to become history.

A Sunday morning sermon at church struck me like a bolt of lightning. The theme was "Guard your thoughts; what you think, you become."

This got my attention because I certainly didn't want to become what was currently in my head. I'd noticed a defensiveness about me, and I didn't like it. This became strikingly obvious one day when a friend joked about something I didn't know.

Without warning, I snapped, "I'm not an idiot!" I startled even myself.

I didn't know where this pent-up emotion was coming from, but I knew in that moment my resentment was still holding me hostage. And I wanted to deal with it before it grew into an even larger monster.

Dr. Case asked me about criticism, and I had to admit how sensitive I was to it. I always had been, to some degree, but my time with Justin exacerbated it tenfold. It felt like I was constantly in a courtroom on the witness stand, having to defend myself. Justin was the one who acted as judge and jury against me—or worse yet, as the attorney who wanted to prosecute me.

Wisdom is the realization that crisis is blessing, and blessing is crisis.

To my surprise, Dr. Case didn't tackle the idea of criticism head-on. Instead she shared some insights about wisdom. "Wisdom is the instantaneous realization that crisis is blessing, and blessing is crisis. God gave us two sides of a brain, and with those parts we judge and seek and crave and compete. Your greatest challenge is to appreciate the way God has made you, regardless of whether anyone else ever does."

In other words, you are who you are. You'll find your greatest balance when you accept those parts of you that you like and strive to become the person you're meant to be, not the person someone else thinks you should be.

All the parts of us—the beautiful parts, the broken parts, the torn-up parts—fit together in some miraculous way to make us unique and worthy and valuable. Just the people God wants us to be. We can only free ourselves of what haunts us when we accept ourselves fully—and when we recognize that God created us intentionally, just as we are. Remember, God doesn't create a mess. Our job is to humbly accept our strengths and to bravely own our weak spots.

So how can we do that?

First, we need to identify our weak spots. After all, we can't remedy a problem if we don't acknowledge there is one.

One of my most glaring weaknesses at that point was my inability to silence Justin's voice in my head. I allowed myself to hear his criticism—still—because in a warped way it was a defense mechanism. Subconsciously I thought that if I prepared myself for what was coming, if I anticipated in my own head what he might yell at me, maybe it wouldn't hurt so much when it happened. Perhaps I could condition myself to cushion the pain.

Your greatest challenge is to appreciate the way God has made you, regardless of whether anyone else ever does.

But thankfully, Dr. Case helped me expunge a lot of the baggage I was still shackling myself to.

This next statement was monumental for me.

"Christi, you have to realize that people live their values," she said.

It sounded good, but I needed more clarification.

"What does that mean?" I asked. "And how does it affect me?"

"It means that people live based on what's important to them. If your friendships are important to you, then you'll make time for them. If your career is most important to you, then that will be your primary focus. Think about it—a while back, peace in the home with Justin was a value to you, so you lived, partly, to keep him happy and avoid arguments."

"Well, isn't that hitting the nail on the head." I was stunned.

Here's where the light really turned on, though.

"You'll be most miserable if you expect other people to live outside their values." She was quite matter of fact about it.

"Let me put it this way," she began. "People draw their own conclusions about you based on their needs and their value systems. They create their own realities, and you're one of their characters. You may never have said or done what Justin accused you of doing, but to some extent, that doesn't matter. He's writing his own screenplay, and you play a role for him. Nothing you do will change that."

"So are you saying I'm wrong to try to defend myself?" I asked.

"No, I'm not saying that. I'm saying that if his value in these destructive moments is to be superior to you—to knock you down a notch or to disrespect you—then your trying to change him in that moment will just cause you angst. You can't change what he values if in that moment he values cutting you down."

"So I'll be most miserable if I try to align his values with my own?" I asked.

Dr. Case paused for a moment. "If you want to control his screenplay or change how he's written your character, you could die trying and never change a thing."

This was huge.

In other words, you can't get caught up in how other people see you, because you can't control that. Their minds are their own territory. They'll see you in whatever way works for them. Even if it doesn't mesh with the way you see yourself. Even if the way they see you isn't a true picture of who you are.

The way someone judges you says more about them than it does about you.

With this revelation under my belt, I knew I had to take control of those voices in my head once and for all. I needed to put a lock on the ugly ones and immediately shift to a kind thought. So I practiced like this: whenever Bitter Betty came to visit my brain, I'd instantly shut her down. If I made a mistake and I started to hear, *You idiot!* I'd shift my thought to *You know, it's not the end of the world.*

One day on my way to work, I realized I'd forgotten a change of clothes for a photo shoot I had. Bitter Betty kicked in: *What's wrong with you? Can't you keep anything straight?* Then I called a time-out with myself. *Let's try that again: Well, it's a good thing I left early today. I have time to turn around and grab them.* Ah, yes. A much more humane conversation. This takes practice, but it works!

Dr. Case left me with several questions for homework, one of which was at the heart of what was still hurting me: *What is the benefit of being criticized?*

This was a torturous twist to take. My insecurities had been digging roots in this part of my self-image for years. Finding benefits to being criticized meant turning some lifelong assumptions upside down. But as I racked my brain, I was shocked to find what came out of the exercise.

The Benefits of Being Criticized

1. It makes me more aware of my own words.
2. It allows me to view myself from a different angle.
3. It helps me see how other people approach something.
4. It helps me to be cognizant of how I approach a person or a situation.

5. It helps me realize I can't please everyone.

6. It helps me see a situation from a different angle.

7. It teaches me what I can and can't change.

8. It helps me recognize that we can see things from different perspectives, but that doesn't mean one of us has to be wrong.

9. It teaches me to be sensitive in ways I haven't been in the past.

10. It teaches me to be introspective, to search myself for what I really believe.

11. It gives me insight into the values of the person who's criticizing me, helping me discern whether he or she is offering constructive criticism or acting out of insecurity or ulterior motives.

"God, please guide my thoughts," I prayed. "Give me wisdom and courage and discernment so I know which thoughts are purposeful and which I should discard. Help me choreograph the images and words in my mind."

The anxiety I had about how other people saw me and about what Justin had said over the years started to evaporate.

I am who I am, I thought. I've had great relationships in the past, and I've had difficult ones. Justin was the most challenging of all, but what he said couldn't define me . . . unless I let it.

And I wasn't about to let it anymore.

CHAPTER 19

FAILURE IS THE OPPORTUNITY
TO BEGIN AGAIN

SEVERAL DAYS AFTER Christmas, I got a phone call from Justin.

"Christi, we're getting audited for the last year we were married. I have the receipts here. Do you want to get together to do this?"

Oh boy. Here we go.

A few days later I was sitting in a restaurant at the Biltmore with Justin.

We shuffled through the receipts we'd kept as we made some small talk.

Then, inevitably, Justin's nastiness came out, and he got back on his high horse about how wrong it was for me to leave him the way I did. He told me that "everyone" thought I cheated on him.

"I don't care what anyone thinks," I told him. "You and I both know why I left, and it had nothing to do with anyone else but us. And for the record, I'll say it again: I did not cheat on you!"

He softened for a minute. "I know."

Let me tell you, I wasn't remotely prepared for what happened next. The bombshell.

"But I cheated on you."

There it was, unsolicited and cold.

I could barely process the statement. Not one word came out of my mouth. For a few moments, everything stopped.

It was like those scenes in the movies where the couple in the middle of the picture is frozen and the world around them blurs into oblivion. There was no longer any buzzing of other conversations or tinkling of silverware on plates. No scent of the salad dressing on the next table or the steaming seafood being prepared close by. All my senses shut down. Just dead silence.

He finally broke my blackout.

"I don't know why I even told you. I guess I wanted to hurt you. Sorry." He shrugged and looked away.

I glanced away for a second myself, trying to absorb what he'd just told me. Then I looked straight back at him.

"Who was it?" I was stone faced.

Oddly, though, even as I asked it, I realized I didn't really care. But frankly I didn't know what else to say. Isn't that the first thing you're supposed to want to know when someone tells you they were unfaithful?

"It doesn't matter."

And he was right. It didn't matter. But true to form, he wasn't going to stop there.

"I remember once we were at a party, and she was there. I was freaking out because I didn't know what to do!"

That image of him sweating bullets and trying to juggle his

wife and his mistress at the same party was actually mildly humorous to me. I had to admit I wondered if she knew how clueless I was. I wondered how she was feeling that night—if she felt bad at all or if she felt betrayed by him.

"You know, Justin," I said, "I guess I'm not surprised. But you're right. It doesn't matter. It's water under the bridge. I don't care to know the details."

We talked a little more about the audit, said good-bye, and left. There wasn't really anything else to say. My head was spinning, and at that point, all I wanted to do was get away from him.

I got into my car and just sat there in the parking lot, dumbfounded.

There was anger, yes. But there was also astonishment. It wasn't the thought that he cheated on me that baffled me. On some level I had suspected it.

What blew my mind was all those years of torment and abuse—all that time I'd listened to him berate me and accuse *me* of cheating, when all the while he was the guilty one.

Here was the ironic part: Justin had admitted to me that he fessed up because he wanted to hurt me. But it turned out it didn't hurt me. It freed me.

In that moment I could truly separate my guilt from my sadness. I still felt bad for hurting him—that would probably never change. But guilt for leaving him? The weight I'd been carrying had finally vanished. His attempt to sink me further had backfired. I was free!

In that moment I had a surprising reaction. It started as a tiny chuckle. Then it grew into a giggle, and a minute later, it was a full-out laugh. There I was, laughing out loud by myself in the driver's seat of the car.

All I could think at that moment was, *Thank You, God!* And then it burst out of my mouth. "Thank You, God, that I'm not in that relationship anymore!"

I admit I was angry, too, but the gratitude was stronger. In fact, gratefulness was oozing out of me. I was almost giddy with it.

Grateful that I'd gotten the courage to leave him.

Grateful that I wasn't tied to him anymore.

And in a strange way, I was grateful, too, that I hadn't found out about this while I was still married to him. Or better yet, when I was leaving him. I was acutely aware that if I'd discovered back then that he'd cheated on me, it would have been my crutch. My excuse not to deal with the real issues.

And make no mistake about it, there were real issues to reconcile.

I would have hidden behind his infidelity as my reason to leave him. I wouldn't have felt the need to do the soul-searching I'd been doing.

How easy would it have been to tell people, "He cheated on me, and that's why I left"? No one would have questioned me further. No one would have blamed me. But I wouldn't have faced the truths that I needed to face. I might not have worked so hard to decipher it all. To examine myself, my motives, my part in what went wrong. To appreciate the pit-filled road I took to get to that point. And perhaps most of all, I might not have implemented the changes necessary to make things right in my life.

The truth is, our marriage didn't crumble because he cheated. It disintegrated for a multitude of reasons—reasons both of us had to own. And only when we owned them could we finally let go of them and move on.

I watched the leaves on a palm tree swaying in the desert air. I fixed my eyes on the sky and said again, "Thank You, God."

And in that moment, I realized something shocking. I could now say, "Thank you," to Justin. Well, I couldn't say it because he wasn't there. And I didn't know if I could actually verbalize those words to his face. But I was getting there.

Our marriage might have failed, but starting that night, I realized it wasn't a complete disaster. We both grew, we both learned, we both survived.

In that moment, I realized something shocking. I could now say, "Thank you."

Henry Ford once said, "Failure is simply the opportunity to begin again, this time more intelligently."

Had I not examined myself and all my broken, warped parts, the "more intelligently" aspect of that statement probably wouldn't have come for a long, long time.

We owe it to ourselves to get real. To live genuinely. Fearlessly. Peacefully.

———◆———

When all is said and done, I really do wish Justin happiness. I hope he can find fulfillment in who he is—in who God has made him to be. I hope he'll be surrounded by the people and the values that are most important to him. That he'll find his best.

Just like I'm striving to find mine.

Because life is too short—and God is too good—to settle for anything less.

Epilogue

FAST-FORWARD TO JUNE 2002, nearly two years after that day when I turned around and walked away from Justin at the airport . . . when I knew in my heart I was saying good-bye. Now here I am on Tunnels Beach in Kauai. To my left is the massive emerald mountain some call Bali Hai, and to my right, about fifty yards down the beach, are sixteen of the people I love most. And far in front of me, the warm, turquoise water laps at the coast.

It's my wedding day.

Dad is at my side as we stand under a canopy of palm trees. "You know, Christi," he says, "you told me once that I'd always be the number one man in your life. I think it's time to change that."

He smiles at me. "It's okay. I'll be second."

I smile back. "No. I'll just have two number one men."

I know now there is room in my heart and my life for all the people who matter to me. No numbering required.

One of those sixteen people waiting for me at the end of the beach is Pete. A man who thinks I'm worth it. A man who was so confident after getting to know me he packed up his Chicago life and moved to Phoenix. A man who patiently waited as I worked to heal my emotional baggage . . . and as I still do. Who supports me, encourages me, and loves me just as I am.

As Dad and I hear the violinist begin to string the melody of Sara Evans's "I Could Not Ask for More," I step barefoot onto the beach, feeling the grainy sand between my toes. I inhale deeply, smiling at the tropical fragrance of sand and orchids and Pacific waters.

And there he is. With each step Pete becomes clearer. He is standing there with an expression that says, "There you are! I've been waiting for you!" He reaches out and takes my hand in his as I let go of Dad's arm. I pass my flowers to Jen, who winks at me. As I glance around, I see Nan, Sam, and Rachel—all with tear-filled eyes and smiles as big as the horizon.

I look into the sky and see that some clouds are moving in. We were told that if it rains during the ceremony, it's actually a wonderful event, signifying abundant blessings for our life together. But let's be honest, I don't know if that's a genuine Hawaiian belief or just a tourist myth they use because it rains like clockwork at this time of day on the north shore.

Either way, our officiant begins the ceremony as I stare into Pete's gorgeous blue eyes. And wouldn't you know, as the ceremony nears the end and Pete says, "I do," a light mist starts to fall. Dad moves in and holds an umbrella over us as we read our vows.

"I looked up the meaning of your name," I say. "*Peter* means 'rock,' and that's exactly what you are to me. You're my rock." I tell him he brings passion and peace to my life and that he'll always be my number one priority. That he's the love of my life and I'll make sure he knows that every day for the rest of his.

I watch this confident, strong, handsome man pull out a card that he wrote his vows on—which makes us all chuckle. He tells me I'm stunning. That he can't help but think of the words *passion*, *soul mate*, and *always* when he sees me. He promises to "make every day of our lives as beautiful as this beach and as you are today."

I am so entranced by him I don't even notice that the rain has stopped and streaks from the sun are peeking back over the horizon.

Then it happens. The officiant says, "I now pronounce you husband and wife." Pete gently places his hand on the back of my neck and pulls me in for a kiss. My heart feels so full I think it will burst open.

Right in this moment, I know I am living a miracle. I am surrounded by people I love, and I get to live my life with a man I trust, respect, and love fully and completely. All is right in the world. I get a second chance.

———•———

One of the most extraordinary moments of the day comes after the ceremony when we're getting pictures taken, just the two of us.

We're sitting in the sand, and I'm leaning into Pete's chest. The sun is setting on the horizon next to the mountain, and the waves are gently lapping near our feet. As Pete holds my hand, I relish this moment—staring at him and absorbing the fact that I'm his wife. He's my husband. Our new adventure has begun. What *was* is behind us. What *is* is in front of us.

Here's the thing: when you get to a point where you're actually experiencing what you wished for but never thought could be, you have to just let it sink in. You have to dive into that moment with both feet and your full heart in it.

To get here, I had to choose forgiveness.

I had to choose to live with an open heart. I had to choose to sit down and shut up and do the work to get to the truth. I had to choose to set boundaries. And I had to choose to live by them.

Just because we can't always see the plan doesn't mean it isn't already in motion.

Just because we don't have answers today doesn't mean they're not coming tomorrow.

And just because we don't feel strong or equipped or self-sufficient right now doesn't mean we don't have it in us to be those things.

When you're stuck in the middle of something painful, it's hard to cling to hope. Not only does it seem impossible, it can also be downright scary. What if what we're hoping for doesn't come true? What if our hope for real love, for a life of freedom and choice, is just an illusion? How can we put ourselves out there like that?

The real question, though, is, how can we not?

We can't let anyone steal our hope, because sometimes hope is all we have. And God wired us with a soul-level need to keep on hoping. Every single day. It's not reserved for people who deserve it somehow. Hope is here for all of us . . . if we'll just choose it.

Hope is God in action. And hope does not disappoint.

Letter to Readers

Dear Readers,

Writing this book has been one of the hardest things I've ever done. It was tough enough to live through it once; the last thing I wanted to do was relive it—in print, no less.

I want to thank you for taking the time to read my story and to tell you how deeply and genuinely I hope it helps you in whatever battle you're facing—whether it's one you're fighting right now or one you've already fought.

I wrote this book for two reasons.

The first reason: you. When I was speaking at a luncheon recently and mentioned I was writing a book about verbal abuse, I was astounded by how many intelligent, capable, kind young women came up to me and said, "Thank you for talking about this." One woman was in the process of attempting to leave an abusive relationship. Another was coping with the loss of a relationship she'd escaped months ago. Yet another nearly brought me to tears when she said, "My dad did this to me. His words nearly broke me." Our backgrounds might be different, our lives might tell different stories, and our pain might come from a different source, but don't we all, in some way, know how piercing it is to feel rejected?

I sit at my news desk time and time again relating accounts of domestic murders, kidnappings, and abuse. After a particularly hideous story about Baby Grace, a little girl who was beaten to death in Texas as her mother stood by, watching her boyfriend kill her daughter, I found myself praying, "God, how do we save these children?" Then it occurred to me—we save their moms. Here's what I mean by that: we make people strong enough, confident enough, aware enough of their value to say no and walk away when they're being mistreated or threatened. We encourage, motivate, and lift up people who feel buried under the weight of loneliness.

I'll bet you know what it's like, on some level, to question your worth. I'm convinced that's why we allow people into our lives who don't belong there. I certainly did. When we feel incapable, overwhelmed, or rejected, attention from anyone can start looking good, and our discernment about who to let in and who to keep out can get muddied. But it doesn't have to be that way. If we can see our own worth, we won't have to look to someone else to give it to us.

The second reason I wrote this: my three daughters. At ages eight, six, and almost three, they light up my world. As I look at their sweet, innocent faces, I'm not foolish enough to think that something like this—being abused in some way in a relationship—will never happen to them. I certainly hope it doesn't, but if it does, I want them to know I've been there, I understand, and they can always count on me.

I will fight with every fierce bone in my body for my girls. And I think you should fight with every fierce bone in your body too—for you. Or for your friend, your daughter, or whoever you know who's living with the pain of abuse. Fight to find healing, understanding, and peace. And, if need be, safety.

Each of us has a different story. Not everyone needs to leave her partner. We don't want to abandon people who need help. Your answer might not be to get out—only you know what's right in your situation. And my purpose isn't to demonize people who are abusive. They're wounded and hurting in their own way. But please hear this: until someone is healthy enough to treat you with civility, dignity, and respect, that person isn't healthy enough to be in your life.

Abusive people need to be willing to do what it takes to own their mistakes and break that cycle. That doesn't mean they have to be perfect. No one is. But they have to be emotionally stable enough to deal with conflict without resorting to abuse. And they have to be willing to get help if they aren't.

If the abusive person in your life can't recognize that he or she needs help or isn't willing to get it, you have every right to leave. When you're in danger, you have every right to get out. Yes, it's excruciating. No one wants to feel as though he or she has abandoned someone. But you deserve happiness and peace. No matter what you've done or where you've been.

This book isn't a fairy tale. It's about a real-life struggle to find my own sense of worth. I can't fight this battle for you. I can't make it sound like this is easy to conquer, because it isn't.

What I can do is commit to being in your corner—rooting for your victory over your own self-doubt. That's what this is really about: discovering your own value in this world.

We can't change what has happened. We can't ignore abuse or deny it or act like it won't happen again. What we can do is see it differently so it doesn't haunt us anymore. Only then will we be able to let go of fear and regret.

Abuse is wrong. Period. Just because you can live beyond it doesn't mean it was all right that it happened. It just means you've discovered the strength you always had but never knew existed.

No one is immune from experiencing a miracle. I'm living proof of that. I spent half of my life subconsciously thinking I wasn't worthy of real love or success. Once I finally fell to my knees in transparent prayer and handed my pain over to God, the light came back on. Finding my faith in its full strength helped me to grasp the courage I'd given up on, even though it was always present. I was the one who gave up on God—He never gave up on me.

There's a miracle just waiting for you to see it on the other side of all of this. I'm not special. It happens to anyone who can learn to live with an open heart again. That's how we're born—open and loving and strong. Even if you don't feel it right now, you are still that way.

My hope is that this journey has helped you find the beautiful person inside you again. My hope for you is big. Hang on to hope, my friends. Hang on to hope.

With love and hugs,
Christi

Exercises and Resources

Let's Get Real:
The Exercises

THESE MENTAL EXERCISES are intended to help you use what hurt you to make you stronger. They take time. You most likely won't finish this in a day or even a week, but don't give up. Take as much time as you need. Use that time for quiet reflection and introspection in your gut. Sit down in a place where you won't be interrupted, and simply get real with yourself. No one else has to see this list, so don't be afraid of being brutally honest with yourself. That honesty, no matter how ugly you might think it is at times, can actually be your springboard to healing.

Now, let me also say this is a practice that helped me immensely, but that doesn't mean it works for everyone. It can be difficult and painful. Don't be too hard on yourself if you can't embrace it right away or if you have to walk away from it for a while and come back later. (Or if you don't come back at all.) That's perfectly up to you. Dr. Case calls me a "digger." I like to be introspective and figure things out. I know not everyone is like that, so cut yourself some slack if you hit a wall.

There are three parts to this exercise: (1) the "Benefiting from the Hurt" list, (2) "The Worst Things Anyone Has Ever Said to Me" list, and (3) your "You" list.

I've included some of my own answers here—the ones I gave when I first made these lists—to help you if you find yourself stuck. I understand. I was stuck, too, at times. It's in those moments when you have to really clear your head and just let answers show up. Concentrate on your experiences, what you've learned from them, and how they've changed you.

Try to come up with at least ten to fifteen answers to each question. But if you have more, *keep going*! It means you're on to something, and that's a good thing.

Your answers can be as simple or profound as you choose. For instance, in asking myself, "What is the benefit of being alone?" I realized I was free to make my own decisions without asking anyone else's permission, and I could listen to whatever music I chose as loudly as I wanted to.

Lastly, I want to encourage you not to be afraid of this. This is about you and what makes you tick. There aren't any definite right or wrong answers.

We all have one life. We owe it to ourselves to gain a profound sense of who we are, discover what's important to us, and feel our place in this world. My wish for you is that you find all those things—and more!

The "Benefiting from the Hurt" List

Imagine something or someone you think caused you pain or problems. Now answer these questions:

1. How did that serve me or give me some benefit or advantage I haven't acknowledged yet?

Note: The benefit of this question is that you can finally stop yourself from experiencing something in a certain way. Sure, if you've had pain, you've had pain. Nothing will change that. However, hidden within the same event that caused you pain, you can also find opportunity, wisdom, and experience of a different kind. These benefits can serve you in a positive way, bringing out meaningful parts of yourself that you can hold on to and acknowledge.

This question helped open my eyes to see and understand that verbal abuse, though painful, was one of my greatest teachers and an important ingredient in the success I now experience.

As you think about the following questions, remember to aim for ten to fifteen answers for each.

How did verbal abuse serve me?

My answer: It made me more mindful of the words I use; it helped me identify and set boundaries; and it made me more independent.

What is the benefit of being alone?

My answer: I have the freedom to set my own schedule; I can find quiet time in the sanctuary of my own home; I can learn to be a "handywoman" and take care of things around the house myself.

How is feeling betrayed helping me?

My answer: I'm learning to depend on myself; I'm learning to better assess who I can and can't trust.

———•———

Again, imagine something or someone you think caused you pain or problems. Now answer these questions:

2. If the painful situation had never happened, what would have been the disadvantage, or what wouldn't have happened that I now value?
Note: The benefit of this question is this—you find out the life you imagined without the painful or problematic person or experience may not be the life you truly want. No matter what has happened to you or who you think has destroyed you, you are a human being with a unique life that is important and purposeful. There is something in you that is deeply satisfying about claiming your life—in all its forms.

This question helped me so much. For years I wished I could pluck certain experiences out of my past, thinking my life would be better without them. Not so. When I worked through these questions, I found out that I want my life—all of it. Who would I be today without a single part?

More questions to ponder:

What would be the drawback if I'd never gone through that abuse/struggle?
My answer: I wouldn't recognize how strong I really was; I wouldn't value those people I can trust as much.

What would be the drawback if I'd never gotten divorced?
My answer: I'd still be in a relationship that most likely would never allow me to be fully me; I'd be beating myself up for staying in a

relationship I knew wasn't good for me, thereby killing my confidence and smothering who I was meant to be; I wouldn't be as empathetic to people who have experienced this same pain.

What would I have missed out on had I stayed in that marriage/ relationship?
My answer: my three beautiful children; a chance to find a healthy, passionate relationship like I have now; the opportunity to follow my own career goals; the glory of living with freedom and an open heart.

———•———

Now imagine either someone you don't like or someone you don't relate to—maybe even someone you despise. Or you may imagine a trait that makes your skin crawl or a trait you feel you don't possess. Then answer this question:

3. How am I like that person, or in what way do I have that trait?
Note: The benefit of this question is that you find out how you really are one of God's many children, with all the same parts and expressions, even if they appear in different forms. It was a hard question for me to answer—maybe the hardest—because I thought I had a fixed idea about what it meant to be something that I perceived I wasn't. This question helped me feel more compassionate toward myself and others, knowing we all have the same traits, that we are all capable of both good and bad.

How am I like _____ [insert name]? (For me it's Justin.)
My answer: I'm ambitious; I care about the quality of the work I do; I care about how people view me.

In what ways am I a _____ *[insert hurtful word]? (For me it's* **whore.***)*
My answer: I have to look good to do my job; I have to schmooze people at work; the more people I connect with, the better the ratings.

In what ways am I fearless? (This is a trait I wished I possessed and didn't think I had until I started this list.)
My answer: I had the courage to leave an abusive relationship; I had the guts to envision a different life—to leave a stable job in Cleveland and embrace a whole new opportunity in the news industry at an entry-level position; I had the confidence to confront, with grace and compassion, a friend who had acted in hurtful ways toward me; I sang the national anthem to a packed house for the Cleveland Indians, even with my knees knocking together from nerves.

"The Worst Things Anyone Has Ever Said to Me" List
Pick out the two worst things per year (all the way back to when you were a child) that anyone has ever said to you. Write them down as quotations, and record who said each comment. (Start with the present time, then move backward. Review the last three years of your life, then three years prior to those three, and so forth until you have gone back as far as you can remember.) Once you've written your list, look for similarities between the comments and separate them into groups that contain similar themes. For example, note the similarities between these three comments:

"You are so stupid."
"You can't possibly think you'll get that job."

"You can hardly balance your checkbook—how do you think you will ever be hired as a manager?"

Answer: they share the idea of doubting the intelligence or mental capability of the accused.

Now use the groups of comments to find out what they mean to you. How did they make you feel, specifically? What did you believe about yourself when you heard comments like these?

After you have a perception of what the comments mean to you, see if you can identify what you believed was missing in yourself. Once you've identified the trait you thought you lacked, you'll find out how you came to value that trait.

This will help you love yourself for who you really are and the purpose you seek to fill.

Note: Here's what I love about this exercise: it shows us what has meaning for us. If something isn't important to us, then we certainly won't get upset or feel insulted by it. Only something that has meaning and value to us will get a reaction out of us—a "charge." So by observing what gets under our skin, we get to know ourselves and find out what is valuable to us. When we take it a step further, we can observe that when we feel something is missing, we seek to gain it.

I take the time to observe what others say that irks me, and since I've been doing this exercise I've learned so much about what I value and also how I want to conduct myself, behave, and think about what I value. Instead of just accusing the other person of being critical or mean, I get to say, "Thank you," for showing me where I think I come up short and stimulating me to be clear about what I value.

I share some of my own examples here. Two people who said things that really hurt me were Eric and Justin.

Eric: He was a high school boyfriend of mine who seemed to pit me against my classmate Felicia. She liked him, he kind of liked her, and she really hated me. I feared he would break up with me and start dating her. After talking to Felicia one afternoon, he came to my house and said, "You're vice president of the class, you're on student council, you've got a ton of friends. You wonder why Felicia hates you? Give someone else a chance, will you? You don't deserve all this!"

How I felt when I heard these comments: I felt hurt, insecure, betrayed, and unworthy. It was the moment I began to believe that if I had too much or was too much, everyone would hate me and I'd be alone.

What it meant to me in terms of how I came up short: I felt I must be ignorant not to see that all I was involved in was causing someone else to hate me. I must be full of myself to have so much in the first place, and I certainly felt undeserving of what I had, because, really, what had I done to deserve any of those good things?

What became important and valuable to me as a result: To be aware of people's feelings, in tune with what's important to them; to live my truest self and recognize my strengths and weaknesses—and to appreciate them; to treasure my friendships more than ever and value honest, loyal people; to be enthusiastic about other people's accomplishments; to not judge other people since we're all battling our own demons on some level.

Justin: Justin was my ex-husband, and there are many examples of moments with him when I felt a "charge" or something hurtful from him. In this instance I was going through a deposition with the attorney for the television station I worked for. I confided in Justin that I was scared. He looked at me, disgusted, and said, "If you can't hack it, you should get out and find something else to do!"

How I felt when I heard these comments: I felt weak, stupid, unsophisticated, and incapable.

What it meant to me in terms of how I came up short: My perception was that I wasn't capable of being a real journalist or having what it takes to be in this business.

What became important and valuable to me as a result: This criticism pushed me to be even more determined and resolute—preparing thoroughly for my job, working long hours, reading and researching before interviews, and learning what criticism to take to heart and what to let roll off my back. I'm actually grateful this happened, because it was a wake-up call for me to grow up and depend on myself.

Your "You" List

Here's where you're going to make a list of what you think is "positive" or "negative" about yourself. Don't worry—no one has to see this except you. I encourage you, though, to be completely honest with yourself. Hey, you've come this far—don't cheat yourself out of a real breakthrough!

The point of this exercise is to use it to see yourself as a whole person, with both positive and negative sides coexisting. When that happens, you'll be relieved to give up harsh judgments of yourself and to stop having the pressure of pride weighing you down.

For the sake of full disclosure, when I did this exercise I was resistant to give up what I thought of as "good things about myself." I thought if I held on to those things, I could fall back on the "Good Christi" when I needed to. But it turns out that if I felt like those good things about myself were really as one sided as I had hoped, the best thing I could be would be self-righteous; the worst thing would be half a person.

After I did this exercise, there was such a sense of relief about being a real person, who, like everyone else, has a mixture of emotions and experiences all happening at once. Somehow this exercise helped me release the pressure to be perfect—to enjoy the willingness to be "just me." I hope you use this exercise to find that same sense of freedom!

———•———

Let's start with a little background. Whether you've studied yourself or not, you have a perception of every personality trait you have. If you like the trait, you likely call it a positive trait. If you don't like the trait, you likely call it a negative trait. (If you *really* don't like a particular trait, you may even deny you have it!) The fact is, every personality trait you have is both positive and negative. The way you label the trait depends on your viewpoint of that trait at a particular moment in time.

This exercise is eye opening and heart opening in the sense that it's an opportunity to find out that you aren't just your personality traits but the sum of all your parts—imperfect ones and all!

My Positive Traits

This is a simple exercise that starts with making a list. Compile ten to twenty positive traits about yourself. I'll list some of mine as an example:

1. I'm a peacemaker.
2. I'm excited to see my kids each day.
3. I have faith in people.
4. I have a sense of style and am comfortable with my appearance.
5. I make good health a priority.

Next write down the negative trait that matches up with the positive. *Don't look for what is negative about the positive trait.* Rather, think about what negative personality trait accompanies the trait you consider positive.

Positive Traits I Perceive about Myself (I'm proud of these.)	Negative Traits That Accompany Those Positive Traits (I'm not so proud of these.)
1. I'm a peacemaker.	I'm impatient when things aren't solved the way I'd like them to be.
2. I'm excited to see my kids each day.	I get short with my girls when they make a big mess.
3. I have faith in people.	I have high expectations of others and get disappointed by those expectations.
4. I have a sense of style and am comfortable with my appearance.	I don't like getting wrinkles or "looking my age." Ha!
5. I make good health a priority.	I don't like the time it takes to work out.

Now let's reverse this exercise!

When you do the converse of this—writing the negative traits about yourself and then finding out the positive trait that matches up with each negative—you find more information to confirm that both the negative and positive do coexist in you. I'll share a few of mine here:

My Negative Traits

1. I'm overly sensitive about how others view me.

2. I allow someone else's thoughts to influence me.

3. I'm critical of myself.

4. I compare myself to others.

5. I'm competitive.

Next write the positive trait that matches up with the negative. Again, don't look for what is positive about the negative trait. Rather, find out what positive personality trait accompanies the trait you consider negative.

Negative Traits I Perceive about Myself (I'm not so proud of these.)	Positive Traits That Accompany Those Negative Traits (I'm proud of these.)
1. I'm overly sensitive about how others view me.	I have a keen sense of what my audience wants or needs.
2. I allow someone else's thoughts to influence me.	I'm humble and willing to pay attention to others' ideas.
3. I'm critical of myself.	I have the urge to get better, to find the best I have to offer.
4. I compare myself to others.	I get great style tips from other women.
5. I'm competitive.	I've learned to use my competitiveness to push myself and fight fear.

When you can get your mind to go back and forth between these two categories more fluidly, you'll find you are neither one trait nor the other all the time; you are a mixture of both. (And if, like me, you're hard on yourself, it's a wonderful feeling to discover that what you've thought of as negative all along also has a positive flip side to it!)

Helpful hint: When you write your list, use your verbs in the following forms: "I am," "I do," and "I have." When I first started this exercise, I did something Dr. Case said everyone she has ever worked with does: I "half owned" my negatives. For example, when I wrote my first list, I heartily wrote, "I am a loyal friend" on my list of positives. However, when I recorded my negatives, I used this verbiage: "I can be selfish." Even the language I used confirmed how I avoided admitting to the negative side of my personality traits.

When you write your list of negatives, write them with gusto! Write, "I'm fussy!" Write, "I'm impatient!" Write, "I'm a perfectionist!" Then ease your mind by finding out what beneficial personality trait you have that coincides with the nasty one. And remember that there is grace enough to cover all the ways we fall short!

Here's the big takeaway. As Dr. Case says, "Neither the positive nor the negative statements are absolute. (In other words, you aren't always 100 percent a peacemaker, and you aren't always 100 percent overly sensitive about how someone views you.) Sometimes you are a troublemaker, and sometimes you don't give a hoot what someone says about you!"

Now it's your turn. Ready, set, *go!* Make your lists. Don't be afraid to be honest. As Eleanor Roosevelt said, "Do what you feel in your heart to be right—for you'll be criticized anyway." And remember: God made you just as you are. Embrace that. He knew what He was doing.

Help for Those Experiencing Abuse

IF YOU ARE being abused and need guidance, here are organizations that can help.

National Domestic Violence Hotline

Advocates are available to you live, twenty-four hours a day, seven days a week. They can offer you a direct link to a domestic violence program in your area.

Phone: 1-800-799-SAFE

Website: www.thehotline.org

National Dating Abuse Helpline

This service aims to help youth and young adults. Advocates are available twenty-four hours a day, seven days a week, via phone, online chat, and text messaging.

Phone: 1-866-331-9474

Texting: Text "loveis" to 77054

Online chat: www.loveisrespect.org

Legal Guidance

WomensLaw.org is a crucial resource if you're in a dangerous relationship and know you have to leave. It lists pivotal information to help you prepare to leave in advance or in a hurry, what to take with you (such as spare car keys, driver's license, money, copies of birth certificates, Social Security cards, medication, and, if possible, evidence of physical abuse), what evidence to keep to prove you've been hurt (such as photographs of bruises or other injuries, torn or bloody clothing, or documentation from police officers or doctors), and how to leave safely with children.

Website: www.womenslaw.org

Red Flags That May Indicate Abusive or Potentially Abusive Behavior

THE FOLLOWING BEHAVIORS are warning signs of abuse, according to the National Domestic Violence Hotline.

1. Jealousy
2. Controlling behavior
3. Quick involvement
4. Unrealistic expectations
5. Isolation
6. Blaming others for problems
7. Blaming others for his or her own feelings
8. Hypersensitivity
9. Cruelty to animals or children
10. "Playful" use of force in sex
11. Verbal abuse
12. Rigid sex roles
13. Dr. Jekyll and Mr. Hyde personality
14. Past battering
15. Threats of violence
16. Breaking or striking objects
17. Any use of force during an argument

Help for Friends and Family
of the Abused

WHAT CAN YOU DO if you suspect or know a friend or family member is in an abusive relationship? The National Domestic Violence Hotline offers these tips.

- Don't be afraid to reach out to a friend who you think needs help. Tell her you're concerned for her safety and want to help.
- Be supportive and listen patiently. Acknowledge her feelings and be respectful of her decisions.
- Help your friend recognize that the abuse is not normal and is *not* her fault. Everyone deserves a healthy, nonviolent relationship.
- Focus on your friend or family member, not the abusive partner. Even if your loved one stays with her partner, it's important she still feels comfortable talking to you about it.
- Connect your friend to resources in the community that can give her information and guidance. (See the list of resources in Appendix 2.)

- Help your friend develop a safety plan.
- If your friend breaks up with the abusive partner, continue to be supportive after the relationship is over.
- Even when you feel like there's nothing you can do, don't forget that by being supportive and caring, you're already doing a lot.
- Don't contact the abuser or publicly post negative things about him online. It will only worsen the situation for your friend.

About the Author

CHRISTI PAUL is an award-winning journalist and national weekday news anchor for CNN's HLN and TruTv's *In Session*. In her eight years at CNN, she has covered a wide variety of stories, including two presidential elections, the Virginia Tech shootings, the Casey Anthony murder trial, the Warren Jeffs polygamy trial, and the Conrad Murray trial. She has also interviewed such noted figures as Senator John McCain, Reverend Jesse Jackson, former drug czar Barry McCaffrey, actresses Jane Seymour and Patricia Heaton, bestselling author Marianne Williamson, and musicians Keith Urban and Jim Brickman, among others.

An accomplished singer, Christi has performed the national anthem for the Cleveland Indians, the Arizona Diamondbacks, the Atlanta Braves, and the Cleveland Cavaliers. She has also performed onstage with Grammy-winning artists Richard Marx and David Foster.

Christi recently became an ambassador for Liz Claiborne's Love Is Not Abuse campaign, which aims to teach teenagers about

dating violence and help them make healthy relationship decisions. She also serves on the board of Safe Kids Georgia.

Christi lives in Atlanta with her husband, Pete, and their three
daughters.